Television
Behind the screen

Peter Fairley

SEVERN HOUSE PUBLISHERS

To My Father

Severn House Publishers Ltd
144–146 New Bond Street
London W.1.
*with grateful acknowledgement to the
co-operation of*
Independent Television Publications Ltd

© Peter Fairley 1976

ISBN: 0 7278 0163 5

Filmset in 'Monophoto' Times 10 on 11 pt by
Richard Clay (The Chaucer Press), Ltd, Bungay, Suffolk
and printed in Great Britain by
Fletcher & Son Ltd, Norwich

Contents

Foreword

by Howard Steele, Director of Engineering, IBA.

I shall always remember my first visit to the BBC Television Studios at Alexandra Palace shortly after the war. I was a schoolboy at the time but the mother of a school friend had a friend, who had a friend, who was a TV Producer. And through him, I got my invitation. I was enthralled. I had never imagined anything like it. I was dazzled.

The heat. The lights. The cameras. The scenery. The cables. Everywhere cables. Gorgeous girls. Bored, yawning scenehands. This is the atmosphere which Peter Fairley has captured so well in this book. The 'sizzle' – not the 'sausage', as someone once put it.

There are many textbooks on television technology. Some good, some bad. Some just plain boring. But there are very few books that have set out to explain in terms that the ordinary interested viewer can understand just what it is like to be present in a television studio. Or a control room. Or, indeed, anywhere else behind the scenes, for that matter. What does the equipment do? How does it work? How *are* television programmes made and transmitted? What's new in the pipeline? And how will the new technologies affect the viewer and his 'quality of life'. All this – and more – is covered by Peter Fairley in the pages which follow.

Anyone seeing Peter Fairley's lucid explanations on television might be excused for thinking that his background must have been in science or engineering. It was not. His background was in English and his training was in journalism. But from an early age he became fascinated by the 'Marvels and Mysteries of Science' and in interpreting his discoveries to others in terms which they could more readily understand. In the modern idiom, I suppose one would call him a 'communicator par excellence' – a builder of bridges between the two cultures.

Occasionally, of course, we engineers wince at some of his explanations and analogies. Sometimes we resent some of the oversimplifications of what we see to be our finest work. But for all our greater depth of technical knowledge and understanding as engineers and scientists, we have to admit that we are not – in general – very good at explaining to the layman what we are doing – or why, how it works and what it will mean to him. Peter Fairley is. He is very good indeed.

Chapter 1
The birth of the box

'Camera One, I want you to pick up Sue as she comes from behind the "flats". Hold her full-frame until she's seated – then zoom in close . . .'

The Director is issuing last-minute instructions from the Control Room.

'Two, we've changed the caption order slightly – I want you to take Caption 3 first, and Caption 2 second. And Three, you now take Caption 1.'

Inside the studio, two cameramen in shirt-sleeves and headphones murmur acknowledgement. A studio hand quickly re-arranges a stack of photographs mounted on cards. These are the 'captions'. Spring clips hold them to black, wooden stands rising up from the studio floor. Each caption has a number.

'Thirty seconds to transmission . . .'

The Production Assistant's voice is deceptively calm. She removes a stop-watch from a cord around her neck and places it with her clip-board of papers on the console. 'Twenty seconds . . .'

'Mike, don't move off those "grouchos" – stay exactly where you are . . .'

Mike, star of the show, carefully places the toes of his shoes back on two small crosses of sticking plaster, marking his position on the studio floor. He clears his throat nervously, reaches for a concealed glass of lime juice. He nods towards Camera Four, knowing the Director in the Control Room will see.

'Fifteen seconds to transmission . . .'

'Ready VTR? OK everyone, settle down. Good luck in the studio . . .'

'Ten, nine, eight . . .' The adrenalin surges. 'Seven, six, five . . .' Heartbeats quicken. 'Roll Telecine . . . Four, three, two, one, go. Grams, fade up . . .'

Cascading figures on a battery of TV monitors in the control room give way to 'titles' identifying the programme. The theme music sounds. In the studio there is total silence.

'Cue Sue . . . Take her One . . .'

The light on Camera One glows red. In the Control Room a similar red light appears under the monitor screen linked to Camera One, showing that it has gone 'live'. Another production is under way.

It is an astonishing fact that in the next second (and every second during which the production lasts) some 2,000,000 electrical pulses will leave the studio, travel down cables, be boosted through amplifiers, encoded, transmitted through antennae, collected by aerials on the tops of houses and finally pieced together in their original form inside

TV sets – 7,200 million signals during a full-length drama or musical, all re-assembled with a timing error of less than a thousandth of a millionth of a second.

That is the miracle of television – and this is the story behind it.

First steps

One day in the summer of 1893, a telegraph operator working in Valencia, Ireland, noticed that his instruments were behaving in a peculiar fashion. The needles indicating signal strengths were jumping about for no apparent reason. The telegraphist – a man named May – checked his wiring circuit but could find nothing wrong. Then he noticed that the needles moved each time a shaft of sunlight fell on the equipment.

He called up other stations to check reception but found that the actual signals, sent to and fro through the atmosphere, were uniformly strong and did not vary. He decided to investigate further. By a process of trial and error, he was able to pinpoint the effect to a number of small components in his equipment made from selenium, an element not unlike sulphur, which was then used for resistances in circuitry. Every time the sun's rays touched the selenium resistances, his indicator needles moved.

Telegraphist May decided to report the matter to his superiors. It was just as well for posterity that he did, for what he had observed was a photo-electric effect – the selenium was offering less resistance to an electric current when in the light than in the dark. After a description had appeared in the *Journal of the Society of Telegraph Engineers*, others were quick to see the implications. . . .

Everything we look at is made up of light and dark shades. Everything the human eye sees is a reflection of those 'lights' and 'darks'. Experimenters a hundred years ago hoped to use selenium as a receptor for light and dark shades and then get it to transmit electrical impulses – in response to those various shades – down a wire.

If that were possible, they reasoned, it might be practicable to make selenium reproduce everyday scenes or pictures *electrically* – the original scene being focused through a lens onto a light-sensitive selenium cell and a black-and-white image of it formed, on some kind of screen, by impulses sent down the wire.

It would be the equivalent of 'telephony with vision' – in other words, television.

Inventors all over Europe and America set to work. The first idea was to connect one large selenium cell and a wire to a screen made up of miniature electric light bulbs. The 'light' and 'shade' impulses, it was hoped, would activate different bulbs in turn, forming a sort of moving 'picture' from the pattern of illuminations. But getting the selenium to send enough current – and vary the strength to match the degrees of blackness or whiteness in the original scene – proved impracticable. The selenium was too sluggish.

The next idea was to mimic the human eye by setting up a mosaic of small selenium cells (equivalent to the retina of the eye), each linked by a wire (equivalent to the optic nerve) to its own electric bulb. In this way, the original scene would be broken up into lots of little bits and each bit transmitted separately – but simultaneously – towards the 'screen' of bulbs. Unfortunately, this also proved impracticable for the very basic reason that nobody succeeded in making a selenium cell produce enough electric current to work one light bulb, much less scores of them. Furthermore, as many as 100,000 bulbs would have been needed to give a reasonable picture.

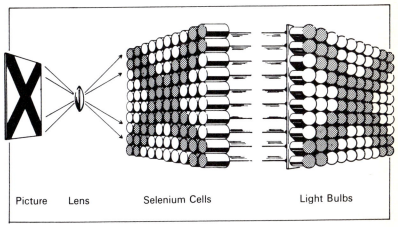

Picture   Lens   Selenium Cells   Light Bulbs

Two English physicists, Ayrton and Perry, next put forward an alternative to light bulbs – magnetic needles, which would move in response to the current reaching them and open or close little apertures. The apertures would let controlled amounts of light through to a sheet of ground glass at the back, on which the 'picture' would be formed.

Unfortunately, this scheme for 'television by wire' failed, too, because not enough current could be generated to operate the needles. A booster, or amplifier, was needed. But none was available at that time.

Ideas were put forward to receive the end picture on a flat, *sensitised* surface, but still selenium proved too inefficient at converting the light into electricity in the first place. In 1888 the German physicist Heinrich Hertz invented the photo-electric cell (which produced current instantly in proportion to the amount of light falling on it) and for a while, engineers tried this instead of selenium: but it too needed an amplifier and none was available just then.

For a decade they floundered. Eventually came the day when an Englishman, Ambrose Fleming, announced the invention of the thermionic diode. Later, de Forest turned the diode into a triode – the first true amplifier. Hopes rose. But even this could not produce the tremendous amplification needed to turn light and shade into a television picture.

It was not until 1923 when two Americans (Jenkins and Moore), two Frenchmen (Holweck and Bélin), and one Scotsman had demonstrated the possibility of transmitting shadows, that the breakthrough came. The Scotsman was John Logie Baird.

The struggles of Baird

John Logie Baird was born in Helensburgh, Dunbartonshire in 1888, the same year that Hertz invented the photo-electric cell. He was the son of a minister, a sickly child, always with pains in his chest. As a lad, he had a curiosity for all things scientific and technical.

The family house in Argyle Street became first the venue for a youngsters' camera club and then the central 'exchange' for a telephone network linking the boys' homes. Wires were stretched across the streets but, unfortunately, these had to be abandoned when a hansom cab driver became entangled in one of the circuits and was pulled from his seat! (The young Baird also installed an electric-light plant in his home, with a dynamo driven by a water-wheel and a bank of accumulators made out of sheet lead and old jam jars.)

As a teenager, Baird started a course in electrical engineering at the Royal Technical College, Glasgow and then went on to Glasgow University. It was there that he produced his first invention – a means of simplifying the mechanisms for electric motors.

His first real job was inauspicious – apprentice engineer in a motor works. But, in his spare time, he read up all the early theories of electrical picture formation and experimented with selenium and photo-electric cells. When war broke out in 1914, he volunteered but was rejected for military service on health grounds. He was given a job, instead, as superintendent at the Clyde Valley Electric Power Company and this enabled him to begin experiments again which led towards television.

The strain of both running the power station and continuing his research – often rising at 5 am – began to take its toll on his health and at the end of the war, Baird took a momentous decision. He quit engineering and went into business.

One of his spare-time inventions was an absorbent sock, warm to the feet in winter but cool in summer, and this he hawked around the clothing shops in Glasgow. He made enough money by personal salesmanship to manufacture and launch a new shoe cleaner, but once again ill-health dogged him.

He decided to go to Trinidad for the sunshine. He became involved in several bizarre business ventures, including jam-making, but then caught malaria and was soon back in Britain, ill and impoverished.

By 1921 he was making soap and had moved to London. But, within a year, poor health again forced him to give up the business and seek warmer temperatures and a slower tempo of life. He moved to Hastings.

All the time, he read technical journals and scientific reports – anything connected with telephony and television. Television obsessed him. He rented an attic over a lock-up shop in Queen's Arcade. Using the few pounds left to him after the soap business folded, he bought some ex-Government wireless equipment. It was to become the basis for the first TV transmitter.

Ronald F Tiltman, a friend of Baird's, describes it thus: *

'Apparatus was almost too dignified a term to apply to the unpromising-looking collection of crude and makeshift objects. . . . An old tea chest, purchased for a few coppers and carried through the Hastings streets, formed a base to carry the motor which rotated the "exploring disc" while an empty biscuit box housed the projection lamp. Scanning discs were cut out of cardboard, and the mountings consisted of darning needles and old scrap timber . . .

'The necessary lenses, on the optical side of the apparatus, were procured from bicycle shops at a cost of fourpence each, while electric motors ready for the scrap heap were pressed into service on duties for which they were never intended and were entirely unsuited . . .

'One or two old hat boxes were utilised, and the whole conglomeration of bits and pieces was precariously held together with glue, sealing wax and odd lengths of string. Over, under and all around the apparatus ran an amazing tangle of wires – wires of all sizes, types and colours, beside which a modern telephone exchange would look simple.'

With this jumble of second-hand parts, Baird set out to achieve what well-endowed inventors and well-supported scientists and engineers on three continents had been trying to do for 50 years – transmit a picture across air.

His reading had led him to the invention of Dr Paul Nipkow, a German scientist who, in 1884, had proposed a system for 'scanning' a picture by breaking it up into small sections. It was known as the Nipkow Disc. Basically, it was a disc punched with a spiral of square holes. This, when revolved in front of a small viewing window – known as the 'scanning frame' – with a light shining through it, had the effect of permitting fragments of the picture to be scanned in sequence through the square holes.

The diagram shows how, when the disc turns, one hole leaves the 'scanning frame' just as the next – punched a little closer to the centre

* *Baird of Television.*

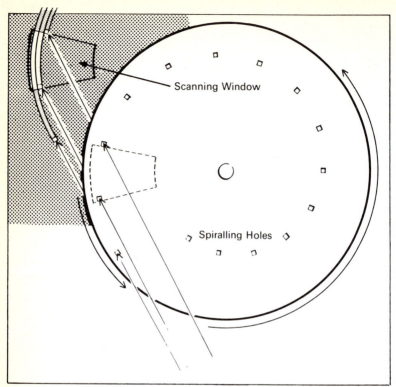

Nipkow Disc

– enters: and as that one leaves, so the next (punched closer still) enters, and so on. A complete revolution of the disc allows the whole picture to be 'scanned' by the beam of light passing through the holes.

In the Nipkow Disc, then, lay the means by which Baird could break up any picture into small, successive pieces of shading information, ready for transmission. Light and dark elements could be shown up through the holes and then made ready for transmission as electrical impulses. An identical disc, revolving at a matching speed at the receiving end, could be used to convert the impulses back into picture information.

Baird decided to punch each disc with 30 holes. These broke up the picture into 30 curved strips of light – or 'lines', as we now call them. He cut them out of cardboard and used darning needles for the axles. It worked. But he still had to find a means of converting the picture elements into electrical signals – and of sending them, either by wire or wireless, across the gap. He also still had to devise a suitable screen at the far end on which the re-converted signals could be displayed as a whole picture. And he had to perfect a way of synchronising the spin-ning of both discs.

He decided to use photo-electric cells to convert the picture into signals. These produced an electric current varying in strength with the strength of the light falling on them – the stronger the light, the stronger the current. The discs, he found, could be synchronised by harnessing two electric motors and driving them in tandem. He decided to use a large ground-glass lens as the receiving screen.

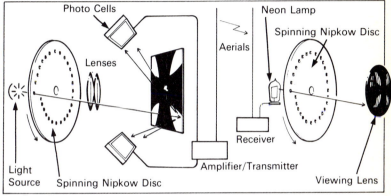

Baird's early transmitting system

Early in 1925, he was able to transmit a picture of sorts along 60 cm of wire. He called it a 'shadowgraph'. At the transmitting end of his apparatus, he fixed a strong light in front of one Nipkow disc with 30 holes cut in it. Light passing through the holes, as they spiralled around, was focused through a pair of cheap lenses onto the target – a picture of a Maltese cross. The beam methodically scanned the black of the cross and its white background as a moving spot of light (nick-named the 'flying spot' in later systems). It was then reflected back off the picture onto the photo-electric cells. The cells gave off an electric current in response to the brightness of the light reaching them – thus, when the 'flying spot' was travelling over black areas of the cross, the current produced was weak; when it struck white areas, the current was strong.

The resultant stream of electrical impulses was then amplified and sent down the wire.

At the far end, the impulses were received by a neon bulb, whose flickerings were in exact response, also, to the strength of the current reaching it. Light from the neon bulb was then beamed through another spinning Nipkow disc, also punched with 30 holes. The darks and lights of the Maltese cross pattern were re-formed, line by line, on the receiving lens at the very end of the apparatus and appeared as a continuous picture.

A few months later, Baird succeeded in dispensing with the wire and the signals went from transmitter to receiver by wire*less* – through 90 cm of air.

Novelist William Le Quex heard about Baird's success and gave this personal description of one of the first-ever TV shows: 'A Maltese cross was first transmitted and was clearly visible all over a large room, standing out luminously from the receiving disc. Other outlines and letters of the alphabet were transmitted with equal success. My fingers, moved up and down in front of the transmitting lens, were clearly seen moving up and down on the receiving disc.

'Those who listen to broadcasting will be amazed at being able to actually see by wireless. Soon we shall be able to both hear and see a thousand miles away.'

Because the neon bulb in Baird's apparatus gave out an orange light, his first TV pictures were not black and white but a fuzzy orange-brown. But they drew considerable excitement from the Press, whom Baird had quickly informed. On the strength of the publicity, the inventor received a gift of £50, sold a one-third interest in his invention for £200 to a cinema proprietor, and was able to transfer all his equipment and belongings to London.

There, he rented another attic, no less shabby, in Frith Street, Soho, and formed a company to develop television. Among those who heard about his activities was Gordon Selfridge Junior, who offered Baird £25 a week for three weeks to give a working demonstration of 'seeing by wireless' in a corner of his Oxford Street department store. This time, instead of the Maltese cross, the inventor used a paper mask with lips that moved, as his picture.

But the passing public looked on it merely as an amusing novelty and soon the £75 paid to Baird by Selfridge was used up on rent and food. In desperation he toured newspaper offices seeking backers, but none was forthcoming. He also offered his patent rights to the Marconi Company, who were not interested. Finally, he turned to his family in Scotland.

To his amazement, they agreed to invest money in the invention and a new company – Baird Television Limited – was formed with £500 capital. Baird resumed research for, by now, rivals were hot on his heels – notably Charles Jenkins in America.

The main problem, at this point, was the light-sensitive cells and their amplifiers – they could show up silhouettes but gave little impression of light and dark shading when anything three-dimensioned was placed in front of the transmitter.

Working alone, Baird used a ventriloquist's dummy nicknamed 'Bill' as his transmitting object: but, despite frequent tinkering with the equipment, the three-dimensional detail of the face eluded him. Suddenly, on the morning of the fifth Friday in October 1925, his

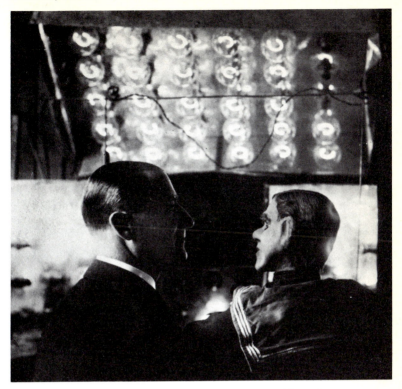

Mr Arther Pruice with the ventriloquist's dummy used by Baird for early tests

modifications paid off. In Baird's own words: 'The dummy's head . . . suddenly showed up on the screen, not as a mere smudge of black and white, but as a real image with details and with gradations of ligh^t and shade. . . .

'I was vastly excited and ran downstairs to obtain a living object. The first person to appear was the office boy from the floor below, a youth named William Taynton, and he, rather reluctantly, consented to subject himself to the experiment. I placed him before the transmitter and went into the next room to see what the screen would show. The screen was entirely blank and no effort of tuning would produce any result. Puzzled and very disappointed, I went back to the transmitter – and there the cause of the failure became at once evident. The boy, scared by the intense white light, had backed away from the transmitter.

'In the excitement of the moment I gave him half a crown and this time he kept his head in the right position. Going again into the next room, I saw his head on the screen quite clearly.'

Baird added: 'It is curious to consider that the first person in the world to be seen by television should have required a bribe to accept that distinction.'

By the following January, Baird had improved his cumbersome apparatus sufficiently to feel confident enough to issue an invitation to members of the Royal Institution of Great Britain to see a 'live' demonstration in his attic. So many accepted that they had to climb the rickety stairs in batches, six at a time. The following morning, *The Times* reported:

'First on a receiver in the same room as the transmitter, then on a portable receiver in another room, the visitors were shown recognisable reception of the movements of the dummy head and of a person speaking. The image, as transmitted, was faint and often blurred, but substantiated a claim that through the "television" (as Mr Baird has named his apparatus) it is possible to transmit and reproduce instantly the details of movement and such things as the play of expression on the face . . .'

The date was 27 January 1926. 'The Box' was born. . . .

Following up the breakthrough

For the next two years, Baird forged ahead, tackling – but not always overcoming – every problem that came in his path. Fresh capital came into his company. He moved from Frith Street to a proper laboratory in Motograph House, off Leicester Square, and took on staff. One of the first technical problems he tackled was the brilliance of the lighting at the transmitter end. Sitters were always complaining of being dazzled by the strong lamps needed to produce a clear image on the receiver.

'I first tried ultra-violet rays,' Baird recalled some years later, 'and several of the staff nearly lost their sight due to their blinding effect! The next effort was to use rays from the other end of the spectrum – so-called infra-red rays. After some trouble, the experiment met with success and I was able, towards the end of 1926, to demonstrate again to the Royal Institution the transmission of a person sitting in total darkness.'

Baird called this development 'Noctovision'.

Other countries, meanwhile, had accelerated their research efforts – notably America. In April 1927, the Bell Telephone Company revealed that it had equipment to transmit pictures down telephone lines – and did so between New York and Washington, following it with a demonstration across 48 kilometres by wireless. Baird replied to this by transmitting pictures between London and Glasgow.

Nine months later he sent pictures from London 4,600 kilometres across the Atlantic to New York. They were picked up on a ground-glass screen measuring only 55 mm × 75 mm but they showed clearly

John Logie Baird testing Noctovision

the ventriloquist's dummy followed by the inventor's head nodding to left and right.

The *New York Times* commented: 'His [Baird's] success deserves to rank with Marconi's sending of the letter S across the Atlantic. . . . As a communication, Marconi's S was negligible; as a milestone in the onward sweep of radio, of epochal importance. And so it is with Baird's first successful effort in trans-Atlantic television. . . . All the more remarkable is Baird's achievement because he matches his inventive wits against the pooled ability and vast resources of the great corporation 'physicists and engineers, thus far with dramatic success.'

A few days later, TV was beamed from London to a liner, the s.s. *Berengeria*, in mid-Atlantic; and then, the next month, sent without any lighting at the transmitter end. The equipment could now respond to daylight.

In July 1928, Baird demonstrated the first colour television – crude and simple, but ahead of the rest of the world. He scanned first through a blue filter, then through a green and then through a red – blending all three to give an image in colour. He chose an audience of scientists in Glasgow for this demonstration. Soon afterwards, a Television Society of Great Britain was formed with Lord Haldane as its President.

But the British Broadcasting Corporation – then less than six years old – waited on the sidelines, so to speak, as far as television was concerned.

One reason was that its technical advisers were concerned about the narrowness of the band of medium-wave frequencies available then for the transmission of TV. Clear, detailed pictures would require a wide band of frequencies. For a TV station to be efficient on the medium waveband might mean it occupying more of the waveband than all the current radio broadcasting stations put together, plus all ship radio stations.

As a result of this limitation over frequencies, only one human face could be shown on the screen at a time. And the screen itself was barely half the size of a postcard. Subjects sitting in front of the camera were allowed to make only small movements (if they were to stay in vision) and there was no sound at all. In the words of one critic, faces were 'curiously ape-like, decapitated at the chin and swaying up and down in a streaky stream of yellow light.' And, in the words of the then Chief Engineer at the BBC, a TV service using Baird's equipment at that time would have been 'an insult to the public'.

Baird, however, persevered in private. At a meeting of the Television Society on 12 December 1928 he announced that he would transmit one hour of television at midnight that night and give further transmissions at midnight every Tuesday and Saturday.

Baird television receiver, 1928

He had his own 250 watt transmitter and his own studio – known as 2 TV – at 133 Long Acre. The picture went out on a wavelength of 200 metres and the sound on 250 metres and probably only a few hundred people within about 8 kilometres of Central London could pick up the broadcasts: nevertheless, he tried to make them entertaining. The 'Baird Concert Party' featured regularly.

American broadcasting companies were less cautious. By the end of 1928, twenty-two experimental TV stations had taken out licences and two – the General Electric Co and American Telephone and Telegraph Co – were actually transmitting programmes using Baird-type equipment. There were no receivers on the market but amateurs made them up at home from parts bought in radio shops.

A marriage was arranged on television. The bride, Bessie Simpson, stood in one studio at the New York Radio World's Fair. The groom, Robert Phylysson, stood in a studio 360 metres away. The minister stood in his home at Yonkers in New York State. TV transmitters were installed at all three points and the vows and blessings were broadcast.

Baird signed an agreement with a group of US firms to exploit his system on the American continent and a new company, Baird International Television Ltd, was floated with £700,000 capital and Lord Ampthill as Chairman.

The inventor had little interest in the financial ramifications of business, so long as he, himself, was clear of the bread line. 'I was busy with wheels and pulleys,' he wrote later, 'and soon came to regard Board Meetings as analogous to going to church – functions to be slept through. Sometimes I awoke with a start at some of the proceedings of these meetings, but after a few questions I relapsed again into dreams of further permutations and combinations of wire and mirror drums and lamps.'

It is easy, more than 50 years after the event, to criticise Baird for moving too fast. He was at the height of his success, his health much improved, his brain sharper than ever. But he did not stop, then, to question the basic principles of his system – a purely mechanical system, with a limitation on the number of lines of light and shade into which a picture could be broken down and re-constructed – nor whether there might be better alternatives using different principles.

Electronic television

While he and his supporters were battling away to persuade the BBC to begin public transmission of television, scientists and engineers working for companies like EMI and Marconi in Britain, and the Radio Corporation of America, were researching and experimenting with an entirely different approach – electronic television.

For a long time, their efforts remained secret. Baird, supported by the Post Office, was eventually allowed to install his system in the BBC studio at Savoy Hill (and later in the brand-new Broadcasting House at 16 Portland Place) and 'out of hours' TV broadcasting began at 11 a.m. on 30 September 1929. Sydney Howard, the comedian, and Lulu Stanley, the singer, were two of the performers and their faces were televised in silence for two minutes, after which their jokes and songs were transmitted in sound only (two transmitters were needed to carry both sound and vision and the BBC then only had one).

Baird himself later estimated that the first BBC broadcast was seen on no more than 29 sets.

Simultaneous sound-and-vision transmissions did not begin until 30 March the following year, when the BBC opened its Brookman's Park transmitter. This time, Gracie Fields performed 'live' and *The Times* reported: 'The future of the broadcasting of television in this country is difficult to foresee. At present, the material that can be transmitted is naturally limited and televising such an event as the Boat Race is out of the question. But it is important to note and register appreciation of the important progress that has been made by Mr Baird in his efforts to bring about television in the home.'

Television sets, such as were used, were then being sold for 25 guineas. But the price later rose to £80 or even £100 and it was not until 1939 that it dropped again to around £40. Baird himself reported in January 1931 that the number of sets sold was actually less than a thousand, although probably 10 times as many had been constructed at home.

Some idea of the suspicion engendered by the new medium inside the BBC may be gleaned from an internal memo sent on 18 December 1929 between two BBC executives – R Gambier-Parry, the Information Executive, to W E Gladstone Murray, Assistant Controller in charge of Public Relations. This revealed that Baird's development company had been informed that, if full sound-and-vision programmes were to be transmitted, 'they would have to be subject to rigorous censorship by ourselves and submitted to me at least two weeks ahead.'

The memo stated that Baird had offered, in response, to give even longer notice of programmes than two weeks 'but I did not want this as I was anxious to avoid any excuse for including his programmes in the *Radio Times*.'

Furthermore, the *BBC Yearbook* for 1931 made no reference to March 30 as the milestone of the first sound-and-vision broadcast nor to the fact that the Prime Minister, Ramsay Macdonald, had had a 'televisor' specially installed at No. 10 Downing Street to view it.

A drum of mirrors

Baird dared not stop to investigate high-definition methods of producing television – he had to make what he could of his low-definition system and exploit it fast in order to attract public attention. To improve quality, he substituted a drum of mirrors for the Nipkow disc (the drum had actually been in experimental use in Germany for several years). And it was this which enabled Baird and the BBC to mount the first 'live' outside broadcast – the Epsom Derby of 1931.

The drum, like the disc, had a 30-line capability – 30 mirrors, each set at a slightly different angle from its predecessor, were mounted around the periphery like the paddles of a water-wheel. As the drum revolved at high speed, each mirror scanned the scene in front of the camera in strips – just like the Nipkow disc – and then reflected the 'lights' and 'darks' at an angle through a lens and on to photo-electric cells, prior to transmission. A similar drum re-constituted the picture on a screen at the other end.

Baird fitted his new mirror-drum equipment into a van and drove to Epsom, parking opposite the winning post. The transmitter was connected to a GPO telephone line, which relayed the TV to his laboratory in Long Acre, whence the BBC took over, pumping out the race scenes through the Brookman's Park transmitter.

Those viewers rich or adventurous enough to own sets were treated to a commentator describing the race, from Tattenham Corner

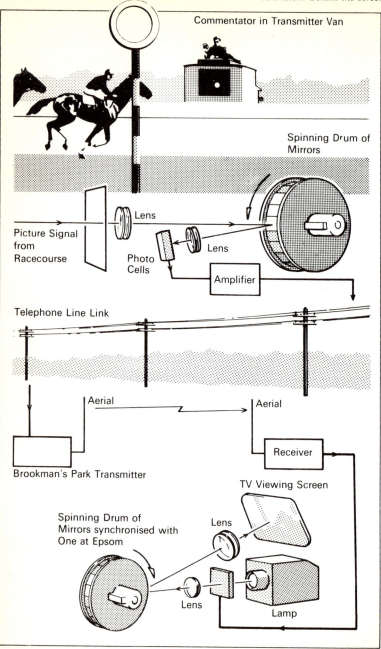

Commentator in Transmitter Van

Spinning Drum of Mirrors

Lens

Picture Signal from Racecourse

Photo Cells

Lens

Amplifier

Telephone Line Link

Aerial

Aerial

Receiver

Brookman's Park Transmitter

TV Viewing Screen

Spinning Drum of Mirrors synchronised with One at Epsom

Lens

Lens

Lamp

How the Derby was televised in 1931

onwards, and a blurred vision of the first three horses past the winning post – Cameronian, Orpen and Sandwich, in that order.

The Derby Day broadcast did much to stimulate interest in TV because it indicated how many outdoor occasions could be brought within reach of tens of thousands of people without their moving from their firesides. *The Times* observed: 'We have found the stepping stone to a new era in which mechanical eyes will see for us great events as they happen and convey them to us at our homes.'

Baird tried out a large TV screen on the public – 150 cm × 60 cm – made up from 2,000 tiny filament lamps: it was demonstrated for a fortnight as part of the London Coliseum show and George Robey, the comedian, helped in the demonstration. This was followed by 'zone television', with even more light bulbs and as many as eight people projected full-length on to the screen – one of them being the England batsman Herbert Strudwick, who gave a cricket lesson.

None of these gimmicks took the development of television any further. But they did attract public interest.

Much more significant were a series of experiments, which both Baird's and the BBC's own team of engineers carried out in 1931 and early in 1932, into television transmission on a new waveband – ultra-short-wave. These opened the door to clearer and steadier pictures.

The more information you wish to broadcast, the wider the band of signals you need to carry the information through the air. Pictures containing a large amount of detail – in other words, a large amount of information – require a wider band than very simple pictures: high-definition TV requires more 'airspace' than low definition. The only way to cope with such a wide 'spread' is by raising the frequency of the transmitter carrier wave on whose back the signals ride. Even by 1932, the medium waveband of broadcasting frequencies was crowded. Television would have completely taken the waveband over, ousting all radio broadcasts. But the ultra-short waveband was vacant.

Moving to it required a considerable advance in transmitter design. But, by 29 April 1932, the British teams were able to announce another 'world first' – the first demonstration of ultra-short wave television. The Post Office allocated a separate wavelength for 'u.s.w.' experiments and from that winter onwards, Baird and the BBC began to co-operate properly.

The BBC's engineers, however, always maintained a cautious attitude to the Baird system of 'mechanical' television. For a TV picture to be satisfactory to the human eye, it needs to be broken down and analysed into at least 100,000 (and preferably 200,000) separate picture elements. This means that it must be divided into several hundred 'lines', or scanning sequences, and for this the Nipkow discs would have needed several hundred, precisely-located apertures. Baird's had just 30. And in an agreement signed in 1932 between the BBC and Baird, under which the Baird Television Company would equip a studio in Broadcasting House and the BBC would put out a one-hour TV programme each week, the BBC advisers insisted on a clause being inserted: 'We should be free to give transmission by *other* Television methods, whether the Baird transmissions continue or not.'

There were 76 experimental BBC transmissions in 1932 and 208 in 1933. Among the latter were a TV review, *Looking In* (presented by John Watt and Harry S Pepper and including Anona Winn as one of the cast), animal programmes about sea lions and greyhounds, and a

Here's Looking At You – *a scene from the world's first high-definition TV programme, 1936*

boxing contest. But still the British public failed to enthuse on a grand scale and buy 'televisors'. Not surprisingly, the BBC limited its spending on the new medium – including transmission costs, studios, artists, scenery and costume – to £2,225 in 1932, £7,129 in 1933 and back to £6,617 in 1934.

Predictably, on 31 March 1934, the axe fell on Baird. The BBC terminated its agreement with him.

Electronic rivals

At about the time Baird and his schoolboy pals were fixing up their primitive telephone lines between houses in Helensburgh, a German physicist called Karl Ferdinand Braun was experimenting with a large glass tube containing a gas at low pressure. Through the gas, from time to time, he fired a thin beam of electrons – negatively-charged particles from the negative electrode of his apparatus, travelling at fantastic speed and suddenly 'bending' sideways or upwards whenever he applied a voltage across an electro-magnet inside the tube. The electrons – known as 'cathode rays' – were deflected on to a fluorescent screen, which glowed brightly with patterns traced out by the beam.

Braun drew heavily on research done by two English scientists, Sir William Crookes and J J Thomson, but by the end of 1897 he could claim to have produced the first efficient cathode-ray tube in the world.

His invention was seized on by a Russian, Boris Rosing, working in St Petersburg, who then proceeded to use it in the design of an 'electron-ic' television system. He envisaged two drums of mirrors scanning the target, their light being reflected on to a photo-electric cell and the resultant electrical energy being 'sprayed' through a cathode-ray tube at the far end to produce the picture. Unfortunately, all Rosing achieved were some crude, geometrical, shapes because he lacked the means to amplify the signals after they left the photo-electric cell.

So did A A Campbell-Swinton, an Englishman who suggested the idea of using *two* cathode-ray tubes – one in the camera, the other at the receiving end. This, he thought (and he called it 'an idea only'), should permit high-definition pictures.

In June 1908, Campbell-Swinton published a prophetic letter in the scientific journal *Nature*. It read:

DISTANT ELECTRIC VISION

'. . . This part of the problem of obtaining distant electric vision can probably be solved by the employment of two beams of cathode rays (one at the transmitting and one at the receiving station) synchronously deflected by the varying fields of two electromagnets . . . so that the two beams are caused to sweep synchronously over the whole of the required surfaces within the one-tenth of a second necessary to take advantage of visual persistence.

'Indeed, so far as the receiving apparatus is concerned, the moving cathode beam has only to be arranged to impinge on a sufficiently sensitive fluorescent screen and given suitable variations in its intensity to obtain the desired results.

'*The real difficulties lie in devising an efficient transmitter* which, under the influence of light and shade, shall sufficiently vary the transmitted electric current so as to produce the necessary alterations in the intensity of the cathode beam of the receiver, *and further in making the transmitter sufficiently rapid in its action to respond to the 160,000 variations per second that are necessary as a minimum.*'

Baird was just 20 when that was written.

The thermionic amplifier tube, invented the previous year, had not been improved sufficiently at that stage to boost the very weak signals coming out of a photo-electric cell and turn them into useful television signals. But it was not long before the necessary improvements *did* come. Also, at about that time, several of Professor Rosing's pupils fled to foreign lands to escape the Bolshevik Revolution in Russia – among them a brilliant young physicist, Vladimir Zworykin.

Zworykin was convinced from the start that fast-moving beams of electrons held the key to good-quality television because they could be made to break up and re-form pictures into literally hundreds of lines, at tremendous speed, giving much more detail than the favoured Nipkow discs (which were never able to achieve more than 240 lines at best) or the mirror drums.

Zworykin joined the Westinghouse Electric and Manufacturing Co in America but later, at the invitation of president David Sarnoff, transferred his research to the much larger laboratories of the Radio Corporation of America. In 1925, he applied for a patent for a new kind of camera – the Iconoscope – and it was this which enthused Sarnoff.

The Iconoscope was about 100,000 times more sensitive than Baird's cameras. A full explanation of how electronic TV cameras work will be given in the next chapter. Suffice it here to say that Zworykin's used a principle known as 'charge storage' which has since become one of the fundamentals of modern television.

For various reasons, Zworykin's main patent was not granted until 1928. By then, one of his former colleagues from Russia – Isaac Shoenberg – had started research on electronic television in Britain under the wing of the Marconi Company. Subsequently he joined EMI Ltd.

Shoenberg and a brilliant team of engineers took Zworykin's basic invention and improved on it. One of the problems with the Iconoscope had been uneven shading in the picture and 'flare' (white glow) due to interference inside the camera. The EMI workers overcame this by designing ingenious circuits to deal with the spurious signals and produced a different kind of camera – known as the 'orthicon'. Exactly which team made the greater contribution to present-day TV has been a matter for argument ever since.

Zworykin demonstrated all-electric television to the Institute of Radio Engineers at Rochester, New York on 18 November 1929. EMI offered *its* version of high-definition, electronic television to a closed audience of BBC engineers in November 1932. Afterwards the BBC's chief engineer, Noel Ashbridge, reported that although the pictures were 'hardly likely, at the present stage of development, to command sustained attention over long periods, they represent by far the best wireless television I have ever seen and are probably as good as, or better than, anything that has been produced anywhere in the world.'

But Baird was not yet beaten. During the course of 1933 he tried a new kind of mechanical technique known as the 'intermediate film process' of television. In this, a 17.5 millimetre film was taken by a film camera in the studio and fed continuously – as a moving belt – into a developing tank, then into a washing tank, then into a fixing tank and finally into another washing tank. The whole process took about a minute. While the film was still wet, it was scanned by a disc spinning 100 revolutions a second and then transmitted in the conventional way.

This called for considerable care on the part of the performers. The time lag meant that announcers had to 'ad lib' for at least 60 seconds after a programme started – and stars could nip out of the studio to a receiver just in time to see the end of their act! Heavy make-up was also needed. The equipment was so clumsy that even Baird could see it had little future. So he then did a remarkable thing – he borrowed, under licence from America, an electronic system developed by one of Zworykin's rivals, an engineer named Philo Farnsworth. He also used cathode ray tubes, obtained from the General Electric Co, in his receivers.

The Farnsworth tube was known as an 'image dissector' and it gave good, clear pictures providing the light level in the studio was good. Baird had almost completed installing the system in a studio on the eighth floor of Broadcasting House when the BBC decided to close down 'experimental TV'.

Rivalry between Baird and EMI became intense. On 5 April 1934, a crucial meeting took place in St Martin's-le-Grand between re-presentatives of the BBC and the Post Office at which the merits and disadvantages of the two systems were compared.

It was noted that while EMI was producing 'well-constructed and workmanlike apparatus' much of Baird's was 'distinctly amateurish in construction and finish'. At the end, it was decided that a Government committee should be set up to consider the whole future of television.

The committee, under Lord Selsdon, sat for six months. It issued its report in January 1935, concluding that 'while low-definition television has been the path along which the infant steps of the art have naturally tended and, while this form of television doubtless still affords scientific interest to wireless experimenters and may even possess some entertainment value for a limited number of others, we are satisfied that a service of this type would fail to secure the sustained interest of the public generally. We do not, therefore, favour the adoption of any low-definition system of television for a regular public service.'

The committee added that results with cathode ray systems were of such improved quality that a public TV service was, from then on, justified. Pictures should have a definition of at least 240 lines and should be transmitted at the rate of at least 25 a second.

The report was a blow to Baird's personal pride. The system into which he had put most of his pioneering effort had lost out on technical grounds. It must have seemed like an epitaph when, on 30 August 1935, the *Radio Times* printed the following announcement

EXIT 30-LINE

'Low-definition television is coming to an end. Authority has now been given to place orders for high-definition apparatus for the London Station at Alexandra Palace, and the present 30-line service is to be closed down. The last transmission will be that of Wednesday September 11.'

Nevertheless, Baird persevered. When the world's first official TV service opened on 23 March 1935, his Farnsworth-type electronic camera stood in covers in a studio at Crystal Palace while its EMI-Marconi rival brought the picture from Alexandra Palace to British screens. But the following week it was *his* turn and, for a while, the two systems alternated.

Nevertheless, the 'Emitron', as EMI-Marconi's camera was called, could produce 25 pictures a second, each made up of 405 lines, whereas Baird's could only form 25 a second composed of 240 lines. It was soon clear which the public preferred.

The demise of the Baird Television Co was hastened by the disastrous fire which burned down Crystal Palace on 30 November 1936 – much of the company's equipment was destroyed. Baird himself went back to the laboratory and concentrated on colour television and on 'television discs' – grooved discs on which TV could be recorded – and worked in comparative obscurity for the next decade.

He died at his home in Bexhill-on-Sea, Sussex on 14 June 1946, with British television firmly established as the best in the world. He left just £7,000.

Chapter 2
Faces on the screen

The first thing the TV camera does when it looks at the face of Andrew Gardner – or Reginald Bosanquet, Robin Day, the Prime Minister, me or you for that matter – is to turn it upside down. The camera lens inverts everything it sees.

The upturned image, if it is one of the latest colour cameras, then travels inside, through a prism, to three glass tubes – one with a red filter over it, another with a blue, the third with a green. Some cameras have a fourth tube exclusively for black and white.

Once inside the tubes, faithful electrical reproductions of the face – and everything else the camera sees – are made and converted into signals which are then beamed out from the studio to the TV set at home. It all happens in a tiny fraction of a second.

Not one but 25 separate pictures have to be created *every second*. They are, indeed, separated – the screen goes blank for a fraction of a second between each – but, because they follow each other so closely, the human eye cannot detect the gap and sees them as one continuously-moving image (the cinema screen shows 24 pictures a second).

Secondly, part of the televising process involves creating little electrical circuits inside the camera at the rate of 8,193,750 a second! This is done by moving beams of electrons about inside the camera tubes, each electron travelling almost at the speed of light and weighing less than .00000000000000000000000001 of a gramme!

Some of the wires used inside the latest colour cameras are thinner than a human hair, yet fixed with a precision of within 25 millimetres. Small wonder then, that the modern colour TV camera costs (at 1975 prices) around £20,000. Yet many BBC and ITV studios use four or even five cameras in one production.

Each camera today has its own viewfinder – a miniature TV screen at the back, on which the cameraman can 'frame up' the scene in front of him. There are also a number of hand controls and knobs with which he can make adjustments.

He can 'pull out' to reveal virtually the whole studio or 'zoom in' to take a head, or some other object, in close-up. The resolution of a modern BBC or ITV studio camera is good enough to show up pores in the skin or the tip of a pin a metre or so away. The focal length of the latest lens gives a flexibility from one metre to infinity although by fitting extra lenses more detailed close-ups can be obtained.

By loading special filters into the front of the camera before going on the air, it is possible to bring extra sparkle to objects, soften their outlines, or give them greater 'depth'.

Extra sparkle can be given by a 'star filter'. This is either a square or round slide of glass which slips into the camera and heightens the reflections off objects in the studio – such as jewellery, mirrors, chrome plate, sequins or shiny plastic. It literally makes the camera 'see stars' – the spangle of stars sometimes appears to glint across the whole picture on the screen. Such a device is often used to heighten the visual appeal of a musical show such as *Top of the Pops*.

Backgrounds can be made indistinct by fitting a neutral density filter and increasing the aperture of the camera lens. All broadcast TV cameras have adjustable apertures so that they can adjust to any lighting condition.

Besides filters, the studio cameraman has a number of other arrows to his bow. His camera pedestal allows adjustment to the *angle* of his shot – he may crouch low, with his lens a mere 60 centimetres off the ground, or leap high, with his lens pointing sharply down from two metres in the air. A foot pump used to be needed to raise the camera; nowadays, cylinders of compressed gas are fitted which balance the weight of the camera so that it can be raised or lowered with a light touch.

Some cameras are mounted on 'dollies', wheeled trucks which can be moved quickly from one part of the studio to the other, or pushed about to follow the pacing of an actor as the camera 'tracks' him. Others are fixed to cranes – very large dollies with counter-balanced jibs to allow the camera to look in any direction.

From the back of most studio cameras projects a long metal handle. This is gripped with the hand to give the cameraman leverage, so that he can 'pan' (point left or right) or 'tilt' (point up and down). Towards the end of this handle is a twist-grip, which varies the focal length of the camera. This allows him to 'zoom in' or 'zoom out' swiftly, guaranteeing him sharp focus all the way to his subject.

Modern studio cameras also have a locking device which allows the operator to pre-set certain shots so that, when a button is pressed, the camera will immediately adjust to the correct composition and focal length for those shots. This is particularly valuable in fast-moving productions such as news bulletins, where one camera may suddenly have to look at a map and another may be trying to overprint the correct positions and names of towns – the two shots being superimposed, one on top of the other.

Another useful facility is a switch, which allows the cameraman to see in *his* viewfinder the shot which another camera in the studio is transmitting at that moment. He can, thus, prepare his own shot to match up with the other man's before going 'live'. This is particularly helpful in drama productions.

To guide him through the order of shots, each cameraman has a 'crib card' – a typed or hand-written list of the sequence of events – which he clips to the rear or side of his camera and glances at from time to time. Other instructions come to him over the inter-comm. from the Control Room. During transmission, the cameraman always wears his earphones, nicknamed 'cans', so that he can hear the director's instructions.

Inside the camera

The colour camera most widely used in BBC and ITV studios, at present, is called the Plumbicon or Leddicon – because lead plays a vital part in its action.

Each colour camera contains three or four of these glass tubes, each about 25 cm long, 30 mm in diameter and weighing only a few grams. They are marvels of precision engineering.

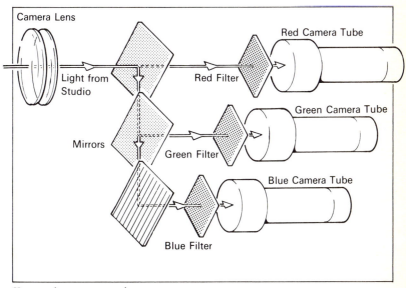

How a colour camera works

The front end of each tube – inside the glass – is coated with a secret mixture containing lead monoxide and lead dioxide. This mixture is photo-resistive – that is to say, its resistance to electricity is lowered when light falls on it (rather in the same way as selenium was observed to behave by May in 1873, except much faster).

The more light that falls on it, the more the resistance is lowered: if the light falls as a pattern, the resistance falls as a pattern across the coating – a cross of light would produce a cross of low resistance, a herring-bone a herring-bone, a circle a circle, and so on.

Since everything which the camera sees is basically a complex pattern of 'lights' and 'darks', the lead monoxide coating faithfully reproduces this as a complex pattern of 'lows' and 'highs', to use the language of electricity.

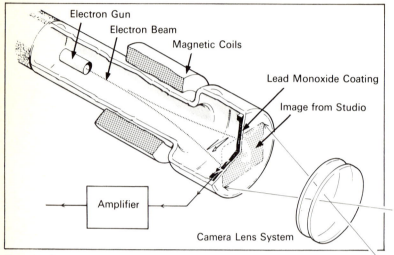

Camera tube

The next thing that happens in the camera tube is that this pattern of resistance is explored from the back, using an electron 'gun'. An electron 'gun' produces, to all intents and purposes, a current of electricity rather as a hose shoots out a jet of water. The individual particles are negatively-charged electrons but they pour out of the gun so close together as to make the 'beam' of electricity virtually continuous.

Being negatively-charged, the particles in this beam head off in search of something positive – in this case, a metal ring encircling the lead monoxide coating. To reach this – rather like sparks trying to jump across the terminals of a car battery – they are obliged to pass through the lead.

The electron 'gun' sweeps across the lead-monoxide coating, with its acquired pattern of resistance, like a hose methodically washing down the side of a car, left to right, top to bottom and then up to the top again, 15,625 side-to-side sweeps every second. For the purpose of this probing, it treats the coating as if it were made up of 625 horizontal lines (405 in the case of black and white TV) with 575 resistance points or 'picture elements' on each line. It thus penetrates 8,193,750 points a second and tries to complete electrical circuits at each point, albeit briefly.

Some of the electrons get through; others are stopped. More get through when the resistance in the lead has been lowered (in other words, where the image coming through from the studio is bright) than when the resistance is high (where the image is dark). Thus Andrew Gardner's bright blue eyes will cause more electrons to go through than his eyebrows!

The passage of electrons through the lead monoxide coating sets up voltages   some large, some small, depending on how many electrons get through. These, too, come out in sequence, to match the pattern of the image in the tube, and they are fed to an amplifier.

Thus, at lightning speed, a visual picture is turned into a series of electrical signals which can be broadcast and re-constituted by receiver sets in millions of homes – to emerge, once again, as a picture. But first, the colour information from each tube has to be combined into one signal and this is done elsewhere in the camera inside a 'colour coder'.

The development of vidicon tubes in the 1960s permitted TV cameras to be made much smaller and lighter in weight. Their predecessors, the Iconoscope and the Image Orthicon, were cumbersome by comparison, although some of the latter are still in use today in other parts of the world.

They worked on a rather different principle called 'secondary emission'. Isaac Shoenberg's team at EMI actually developed the first commercial electronic TV camera, in the early 1930s. They called it the 'Standard Emitron' but the tube inside was very similar to Vladimir Zworykin's Iconoscope. The Emitron was in use at the BBC from 1936 to 1939 and performed memorably during the 'live' outside broadcast of the Coronation of King George VI in 1937.

The old Iconoscope cameras, whilst a great advance over the mechanical-scanning devices used by John Logie Baird, tended to produce a whitish 'flare' along the bottom of the picture, especially in the bottom right-hand corner. These white patches were known as 'shading signals' and elaborate correcting circuits had to be built into the cameras to compensate for them. Furthermore, the Iconoscopes called for fairly strong studio lighting – to the discomfort of performers.

Nevertheless, their basic principle of scanning is still in use in all TV cameras today.

Following the Emitron and the Iconoscope tube came the Orthicon and then the Image Orthicon camera. This contains a glass tube about 50 centimetres long and $11\frac{1}{2}$ centimetres in diameter and is about 1000 times more sensitive than the Iconoscope.

Some Image Orthicon cameras maintained for special uses today are more sensitive even than the human eye.

Lighting

A television studio is not unlike a small factory with heavy equipment on the shop floor and a forest of light, moveable machinery slung from the ceiling – specially-shaped girders, supporting rails, brackets, powerful lamps, microphones, scenery and so forth. Ceilings may be 17 metres or more high.

On the floor – and frequently causing people to trip over them – are cables of every size; hundreds of metres of cables; cables snaking out to cameras, cables feeding microphones, cables connecting lights.

A great deal of time and trouble is taken over lighting, ensuring faithful reproduction of colours, avoiding unwanted shadows and showing up clear details on small objects or faces. Lighting a studio before a production of *Magpie* may take two hours or more; in the case of a song-and-dance 'spectacular', perhaps a whole day.

Lighting is under the control of the Lighting Director or Supervisor, whose vocabulary refers to 'floods', 'spots', 'barndoors', and 'monopoles', to mention just a few terms. Every light seems to have its nickname. The smallest (750 watts) is known as a 'pup'; lamps of a

Under hot studio lights – the BBC 2 **Money Programme** *goes on air*

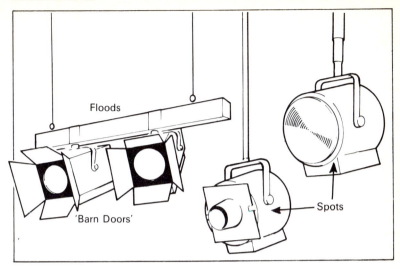

higher power, generating five and 10 kilowatts, are known as '5 k's or '10 k's. Arc lamps are often referred to as 'brutes' and hand-lamps as 'hand-bashers' or 'frizzers'. The moveable flaps over the fronts of lights – which can be adjusted to soften the glare or to give shadow effects – are called 'barndoors'.

The cables or rods from which the ceiling lights are suspended – can be adjusted either manually, using a long pole, or by attaching an electric drill-like device to them, which motors them up or down.

Comparatively small studios, such as those at ITN, may nonetheless have as many as 70 lights mounted in the ceiling whilst those employed for major drama or musical productions at ATV or Granada may have 500 – or in the case of Pinewood Studios – 1000. Some studios have automatic lighting which can be programmed in advance of the show.

The Make-up Department

The nature of the lighting on a 'set' concerns not only the Director but also the make-up department. Often a make-up artist will go into the Control Room at rehearsal time in order to see what effect the lighting is having on the faces of the performers. Then she will return to her bench and take out the necessary sticks, creams and powders to suit each individual's colouring.

In the days of black-and-white television, make-up was primarily corrective – it simply covered up the blemishes or matted down the shine. But with the arrival of colour TV, the art took on a new subtlety. Make-up had to be much finer, more luminous and took longer to apply.

Faces have different shades in them which have to be evened out. A face which looks attractive in black-and-white often appears flat and unnatural in colour. Foundation has to be almost polished into the skin to give a natural shine.

Shadows under the eyes appear more pronounced in colour and have to be lightened. The bones under the eyebrows reflect light and therefore appear larger – making the eyes seem smaller – and so have to be darkened.

The 'five o'clock' shadow, which most men have, looks like two or three days' growth of beard to a colour camera unless camouflaged. Bald heads must be powdered – and covered with make-up like the face, neck, hands and any other part which may show on the screen – to prevent shine.

Dyed-blonde hair has a tendency to give off a lime-green aura. Hair-pieces, unless they are complete wigs, tend to show up as false because they reflect light differently from real hair. Nicotine-stained fingers show up yellow unless made-up.

All reds have to be avoided. Lipstick, if worn, has to be toned down; rouge is given a beige overtone. Performers who drink before going in front of the camera are in danger of looking like beetroots unless camouflaged with make-up. In the early days of colour transmissions, this latter phenomenon used to worry Directors so much that they would insist on actors keeping away from alcohol even during the lunch hour.

The question of TV performers drinking is a sensitive one. There is probably no greater crime in the eyes of those who produce television than slurring your words as an effect of alcohol; yet alcohol does help to relax many who feel nervous in front of the camera.

Most TV studios have a hospitality suite attached – often called the 'Green Room' but rarely coloured green – in which artists and guests can have a drink before going 'on air'. But gauging just how much drink should be allowed for it not to show on the screen is a ticklish business.

Studio illusions

There are many other illusions in television. One of the most common studio illusions is that produced when a picture is projected behind the performer to make it seem as if he is somewhere else than in the studio. Whereas, in the early days, the Director had only scenery or a cloth back-drop to help him create this illusion, today he has a variety of electrical or electronic techniques at his disposal.

The simplest is called 'back-projection'. It calls for a slide or film

Translucent Screen

Actors

TV Camera

Film Projector

Back projection

projector to be set up behind an opaque screen and for the desired scene to be projected on to that screen. The performer then positions himself in front between the screen and TV camera. The TV camera sees the performer *and* the picture behind him as one, creating the illusion that he really is in front of that particular view. The technique is used frequently in series such as *Z Cars* or *Macmillan and Wife* where a lot of car driving is called for: the countryside rolling past in the background is usually on film and the 'car' is static. Often only a section of car is used, with parts cut away, to facilitate the camera shots.

A similar effect is obtained using Eidophor. Eidophor projects television – as opposed to film – on to the screen behind the actor. It consists basically of a large vacuum tube, a lens projector and the screen itself, which may form part of the studio 'set' or be portable.

A more advanced TV projection system is called Advent, invented in America and first used in Britain by Howard Steele, Director of Engineering of the Independent Broadcasting Authority, when he gave the Institution of Electrical Engineers' Faraday Lectures in 1975/76. Advent takes a colour TV signal, passes it through a de-coder and then projects the picture through a cluster of three lenses – red, green and blue – on to the front of a special reflecting screen positioned 3 metres away. It creates much 'sharper' pictures on the screen than any other system so far.

A fourth way of introducing pictures behind the performer is called Chromakey – literally the 'key colour'. Sometimes it is referred to as 'CSO' (Colour Separation Overlay). Chromakey is used every night for both BBC and Independent Television news, as well as in many individual company productions. Whenever a still or moving picture appears behind a newscaster, that is Chromakey in action.

It is a way of 'switching out' one of the three primary colours used in TV (red, green or blue) and replacing it with picture information from a separate source. It may be film which is fed in. It may be video-tape. It may be a still photograph or a 35mm slide. All appear to the viewer as though they were being projected into the studio behind the newscaster's shoulder: in fact, they are being fed into the electronic links between camera and transmitter from elsewhere in the building.

The 'key' colour chosen by ITN for its news bulletins is a rich royal blue. So a royal blue board or screen is placed behind the newsreader, above and to one side of his shoulder. Every time the studio camera sees this colour, a switch is triggered in an electronic 'mixer' outside the studio and the external picture information is fed into the outgoing TV signal instead. A picture, either still or moving, appears to jump into place behind the newscaster and change with each item of news.

To understand the technical principle behind Chromakey, one has to remember that the scene in front of the camera is being scanned all the time by three Plumbicon tubes – one responding to red, one to green, one to blue. The signals from all three tubes are fed into a box of electronics where the red and green signals are inverted and subtracted from the blue.

Obviously, when the scanning beam hits anything in the image which is blue (assuming, that is, that blue has been chosen as the 'key' colour), the blue signal leaps to maximum and the other two to zero. As soon as this happens, a switch in the 'mixer' outside the studio is automatically tripped and a tiny portion of the external picture – which is to appear behind the newscaster – is substituted in the scanning sequence. A whole frame is built up, line by line, 25 frames every second, with the external picture signal nipping in wherever blue registers maximum.

The BBC sometimes uses blue as its 'key' colour, but also uses green or yellow. Blue has the advantage of being a colour of low brightness, so any 'halo' effect around the newscaster when he is sitting in front of the blue board, is therefore dark and relatively inconspicuous. A yellow or green halo tends to be more noticeable. Furthermore, flesh contains very little blue and therefore shows up well against a blue background.

In 1964, long before I had even heard of Chromakey, I took part in a BBC experimental colour programme about fire. Watching the playback of the recording, I noted that blue seemed to be a colour which came through particularly cleanly and pleasantly on television.

So when, four years later, my new masters at ITN switched over from black-and-white transmissions to colour, I decided to invest in a whole lot of blue clothing in the hope of appearing smart on the screen. I bought two blue suits, seven blue shirts, blue ties, blue socks and a blue silk pocket handkerchief.

Then they introduced Chromakey – and I have never been able to wear any of it in the studio since! For, just as the camera switches to external picture signal whenever its scanning beams register the blue screen behind the performer, so it will switch to the external signal if they register something blue on the performer himself. In the studio, you feel and see nothing. But on the screen, film of, say, Chairman Mao's marching hordes appears to be moving right across your chest! This once happened 'on air' to Robin Day when he wore a bow-tie with spots which matched the 'key' colour. Nowadays spare ties, jackets and even shirts are kept handy in some studios in case a performer turns up wearing the wrong colour.

A less complex but often effective way of forming backgrounds is the Cyclorama – or 'cyc' – in TV jargon. This is a shallow, U-shaped construction of plywood, gauze, cloth or canvas, some five metres high and up to 20 metres long. By careful lighting, suitable backgrounds of different colours or moving patterns can be formed on it. If floor and 'cyc' are of the same colour, an illusion of infinite space can be created.

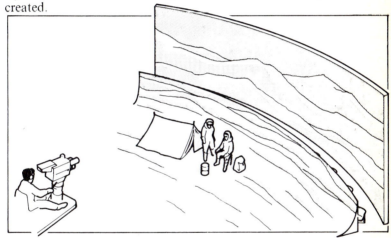

The Cyclorama – 'cyc' for short

A quite different studio illusion is created by two devices called Teleprompter and Autocue. These allow a performer to give the impression that he has memorised his words and is not reading from a script. Actors in drama productions, in many light entertainment shows and in some 'chat shows' *do* memorise their words, of course, but in news and current affairs programmes, prompters are used very frequently.

Autocue was invented first. In the early days, it consisted simply of a wide belt of yellowish paper wound on to two rollers, on which the script could be typed in huge letters. A motorised drive mechanism set it rolling at a speed controlled by an operator, who sat beside the camera. The performer looked at the belt instead of the camera lens and read off the words as they moved in front of him.

Nowadays, Autocue has become more sophisticated. Whereas,

when the belt of paper was set to one side, it used to force the performer to look slightly 'off camera' – an infuriating effect for the viewer – electronics and cunning optics today permit the words to be fed to a TV screen either just below the camera lens or even *around* the camera lens. It becomes almost impossible, therefore, to detect the movement of the performer's eyes as the words roll directly in front of him.

ITN has invented its own form of prompter. Its function is the same as that of Autocue. It consists of a trolley placed in one corner of the studio on which are mounted a steel tube (resembling a small telescope), a shallow metal trough and a winding handle. The script is typed, using an ordinary typewriter, on to a 75 mm-wide roll of white paper. The end of this roll is then placed in the straight metal trough where it is gripped and moved forward through the trough in response to turns of the winding handle.

The operator sits down at the trolley, grips the winding handle in the right hand and presses a foot on a pedal switch. This switches on a light which shines down on to the words on the roll of paper. As she turns the handle to match the newscaster's reading speed, so the words are transferred by a system of lenses in the 'telescope', down cables and on to small screens beneath the camera lenses.

Television prompter in action at ITN . . .

. . . Prompter's words appear on screen below camera lens for Gordon Honeycombe to read

Cables link the system to several cameras simultaneously – enabling a pair of newscasters to move the news reading back and forth slickly between them.

Scripts are usually also supplied in sheet form in case the machine fails, and to enable the Director in the Control Room to gauge how far the reader has progressed. The top copy of the script is known as 'greys' (the paper is usually grey in colour) and is placed on the desk in front of the newscaster. From time to time, he may glance down at it, or perhaps read from it.

Once again, prompters are not employed deliberately to spoof the viewer but in order to make production more efficient. Timing is all-important in television and it is vital that the contents of a programme exactly fill the 'slot' – otherwise the programme will over-run or under-run. The two reading systems help timing and also give confidence to the performer – he knows he is not likely to forget his words. On ITV, this timing is crucial (if a bulletin over-runs by more than about 12 seconds a 'commercial' may have to be dropped, resulting in a loss of anything up to £10,000 to the ITV network). So the words of every page of script are counted, as is the length of every piece of film or video-tape to be shown. Working to a formula that 'it takes the average person an average of one second to read out three average words' it is possible to work out precisely how long each item in the news bulletin should take to read and then check, as the bulletin progresses, that the timings are being adhered to.

Although the prompters or Autocue are delightfully easy to use, they have an interesting psychological effect on the performer: it becomes difficult to 'ad lib' while reading the words, or to mix memorised material with script. Whilst most people who appear regularly in front of the camera can memorise words to a degree – or make chatty, impromptu statements to the camera without faltering – once the words are down for reading the mind seems to lose its freedom. You become mentally committed to the prompter and any error in the words typed or failure in the system causes a brief moment of panic in the brain.

Highly-practised professionals like the BBC or ITN newscasters usually manage to mask this without the viewer noticing. But for those who read a prompter less often – like me – a hiatus can be agonising. I well remember an incident in 1973 when news reached ITN, just before *News at Ten*, that the astronauts inside the Skylab space station had run into problems and were in danger. The Output Editor decided to make the item the No. 1 story in the bulletin.

I hastily wrote a script, handed it to a production assistant for the words to be typed on to the roll of prompter paper and raced down to the studio. The girls who do this typing work at amazing speed and, usually, with great accuracy. Each item gets its own heading (a single word such as 'SKYLAB') to distinguish it from the others and the girls slip into the studio – sometimes only seconds before transmission – to fix it into place in the roll, using scissors and paste.

On this particular occasion – with no rehearsal to show up the mistake – she stuck it in the wrong place. Unaware of her error and without 'greys' as a back-up, I heard Reggie Bosanquet read out a brief introduction to the story and then say 'and now with fuller details, here's our Science Editor, Peter Fairley . . .'

The screen in front of me, carrying the prompter script, started to roll. But instead of the title 'SKYLAB', a different heading leaped into view – 'LONRHO'. What does one do in such circumstances? One coughs, nervously. That gives the brain a second to think. Then one coughs again; two seconds. Suddenly, the memory of what I had written in my Skylab script came back to me and I started to 'ad lib'. Possibly, ten million viewers did not notice; possibly they did, although none rang up to complain. All I remember is the sickening feeling of being caught napping, mentally, and of the micro-second of panic which followed. Had I not used the prompter that night but opted, instead, to 'ad lib' for one and a half minutes – telling the facts from memory – I would probably have given a coherent report. As it was, the memory has become a recurring nightmare and the word 'LONRHO' is seared indelibly across my mind's eye.

Sound reproduction

Sound, of course, is as important as vision. The walls of the TV studios are sound-proofed with padding and acoustic tiles, usually, which are then painted a neutral colour. Silence is important for every type of production because the microphones used in television are extremely sensitive – some could pick up the sound of a pin dropping three metres away.

Whilst the Lighting Supervisor refers to his equipment in nick-names, the Sound Supervisor thinks of *his* in numbers – '224', 'C451', 'C61' or '190' are all abbreviations for types of microphone. There are boom microphones, desk microphones, ribbon microphones, floor microphones, clip-on microphones, lip microphones and radio micro-phones. Each has its own characteristics and is used for a specific situation.

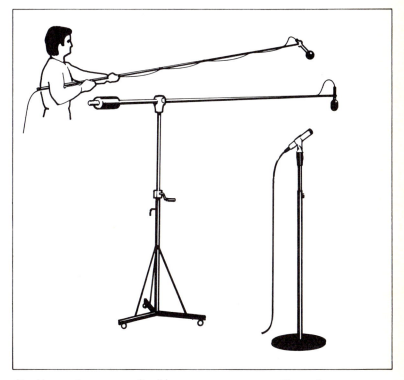

Hand boom mike   Small boom   Floor mike

'Boom mikes' for example, are used mainly in drama productions or programmes where there is a lot of movement. They extend overhead, usually just out of sight, above the artist.

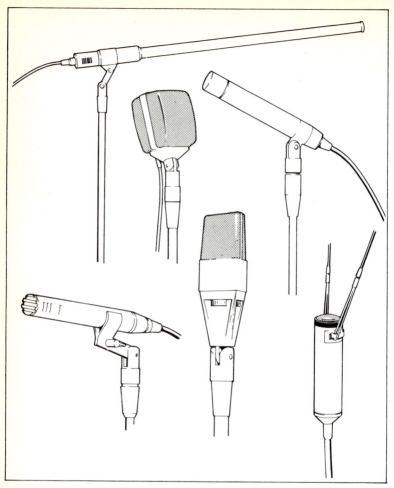

*Microphones. Top left: Directional Dynamic. Top centre: Moving Coil Omni-Directional.
Top right: Directional Mike. Bottom left: Condenser Directional. Bottom centre: Ribbon
Mike. Bottom right: Neck Mike*

Floor and desk mikes are probably the most sensitive – the ones
used for news and current affairs programmes in studios such as ITN's
are known as 'dynamic'. The Sound Supervisor is always very careful
to take a 'voice level' reading from the performer before he goes 'live'
because their sensitivity needs adjustment to suit the individual.

'Clip-on mikes' are particularly useful if the performer has to move
about, or if a boom may cast a shadow. The latest ones are less than
half the length of (and about the same diameter as) a cigarette and
they can be clipped unobtrusively on to a tie, coat lapel or dress – or

hung around the neck on a cord. Wires leading from them may be tucked down trouser legs or skirts.

'Lip mikes' are especially useful for sports commentaries because they have a projecting mouthpiece which cuts down the background noise and shouts from the crowd. But they call for quite a bit of practice, on the part of the commentator, if he is to gauge the level of his voice correctly and avoid too high a pitch.

Many performers would like to use a 'radio mike' which has no trailing wires but a small transmitter (about the size of a pocket calculator) which can be slipped into a pocket. Some radio mikes used by comedians or singers have the transmitter built into the handle and a small aerial wire hanging down about 15 centimetres. The radio mike gives the artist complete freedom to move, but it is expensive (anything up to £500) and needs a special transmitter licence to operate. For these reasons, its use is mainly confined to situations where it is difficult to trail cables. But its development in the 1960s has enabled some spectacular television to be mounted, especially in co-ordination with the zoom lens.

Radio mikes permit all kinds of long 'shots' in drama productions out of doors, conversations from the insides of vehicles and reports from precarious situations such as cliff-faces, gantries, ladders or tall buildings.

How microphones work

What *is* television sound?

Just as it is the camera's job to turn the picture into electricity, so it is the microphone's job to turn sounds into electricity. It does this by picking up vibrations.

All sounds are the result of vibrations, vibrations which travel in waves, radiating outwards like ripples on a pond after a stone has been thrown into it. Different kinds of sound produce different vibrations – high-pitched sounds (such as a whistle blowing) produce high-frequency vibrations, low-pitched sounds (such as a double-bass, a drum or a groan) produce low-frequency vibrations. The human ear can only cope with vibrations rippling with a frequency of between 16 and 16,000 cycles per second.

If an ear is in the way of these vibrations, the ear drum begins to vibrate also. A microphone is an electrical equivalent of the human ear drum.

In place of human tissue, the microphone has a thin metal plate called a diaphragm. This vibrates in response to sound waves striking it. The vibration of the metal disturbs an electrical field set up between two magnets. Changes in voltage occur which can be taken off the microphone terminals by wires, fed to an amplifier and relayed to a transmitter.

The electrical output of the microphone is known as an 'alternating voltage' because it alternates first one way, then in the opposite direction – and it varies in strength and frequency to match the original sound. It is then put on to the back of an electro-magnetic carrier wave, along with the TV picture signal, and radiated out to the world.

In the main, three families of microphone are used in television today – 'ribbon', 'dynamic' and 'condenser'. In physical appearance, a 'ribbon' mike looks rather like a rectangular bar of soap with holes punched in it; a 'dynamic' mike resembles a slender torch with a blob on the end; a 'condenser' mike can be as small as a thumbnail or as large as a torch and, like a torch, is housed in a straight-sided cylinder. 'Ribbon' mikes are bi-directional – speakers can be straight in front or behind. Most mikes of the 'dynamic' variety are omni-directional but some have limitations on the frequency of the sounds they pick up. 'Condenser' mikes are good on all frequencies but many require a power supply.

Ear-pieces

Presenters, newscasters and certain other performers have a link to the Control Room also. Because they appear in vision, headphones are considered unsightly. Instead, an inconspicuous flesh-coloured ear-piece is issued for insertion into the ear-hole. Those who appear frequently, such as newscasters, have special castings taken of their ears: plastic or rubber moulds are then made to fit snugly. The mould is linked by a slim, transparent plastic tube to a midget loudspeaker which is usually strapped to the shirt, mid-way between the shoulder-blades, using sticking plaster. The performer is thus able to get secret instructions during a programme without the viewer noticing.

The ITN newscasters tell the story of how these moulded ear-pieces were introduced in the 1960s. They created a terrible itching – 'sometimes it felt as if fleas were crawling about in your ear-hole during the news' – and suspicion grew that they might be infectious. But sound technicians investigated and discovered that the itching was due to moisture – condensation and sweat – gathering in the ear-hole and becoming trapped under the close-fitting mould.

A small groove is now cut in all such ear-pieces to allow the ear to 'breathe' and there has been no recurrence of the problem.

Down the ear-piece comes what is known, in TV jargon, as 'talk-back' or 'sound'. This may be the sound of a commentary being spoken over a film or video-tape sequence, or spoken instructions from the Control Room. Switches in the Control Room allow the programme director to over-ride anything else being heard in the ear-piece or to speak, selectively, to any performer equipped with one.

Sound effects

But there is more to the story of sound in television than the selection and placing of microphones – there are the sound *effects*.

The BBC and ITV companies have built up vast sound-effects' libraries, on disc, on tape, on cassette or cartridge. Often extra sounds are fed into a production from the 'grams' (short for 'gramophones') department, containing decks of turntables and machines for slotting in cartridges and racks of pre-recorded sounds. The turntables have balanced, lightweight pick-ups which allow the needles to move backwards or forwards in the grooves of a disc without damaging it, so enabling the operator to position the needle very precisely at any point in the sound-effect or piece of music. Several turntables, working simultaneously, allow quite a complex story in sound to be built up to back up a sequence of silent film or video-tape.

It is an open secret in television that many of the sounds of battle during war sequences come out of the sound-effects' library. The purpose is not deliberately to deceive the viewer but simply to make the coverage more acceptable – often the film arrives 'silent', shot with a film camera to which there is no sound attachment, by a lone camera-man in the field. The film would seem remarkably uninteresting if background noises were not added.

Dubbing

Many sequences are 'dubbed' before going on to the screen. 'Dubbing' is done in a 'dubbing suite' and consists of mixing sound-effects and any commentary. If extra sounds are to be added, the film editor usually supplies the Dubbing Mixer with a 'dubbing chart' which guides him as to when and where to add the effects.

A piece of film of, say, an MP arriving at No. 10 Downing Street for a Cabinet Meeting may call for general street noise, the slowing of a car engine, the thud of a car door closing, the echo of footsteps on the pavement – and then the 'natural' sound of the MP saying 'No comment'! All this may have to be mixed together in the dubbing suite, either because two different cameras were used to film the sequence, or because only silent cameras were used, or because the sound recordist at the scene was not in a position to record all the sounds 'cleanly' while the camera was taking pictures.

Sound-effects' libraries are fascinating places. The Dubbing Mixer at Anglia Television, for example, can put his hands on any one of 200 half-hour tapes and 72 cartridges containing such varied effects as sows grunting, earth being knocked from sugar beet, a humane-killer being fired in a slaughter-house, milk bottles being washed, badgers feeding, hedgehogs courting, minks screaming, a Siamese kitten miaowing and a baby seal waddling on pebbles.

Other indexes include aeroplane dog-fights, a hub-cap falling off a

car, eggs frying, a pea-cleaner, raucous laughter from men, the inside
of a beehive and Chinamen talking in the distance!

The production team

Behind every face on the screen, there is a minimum of 14 people
directly involved in putting it there. Sometimes, in a large production,
as many as 100 may be at work.

The nation-wide children's programme *Magpie*, for example, has a
50-strong Thames Television production team supporting its three
presenters each week. These include seven working the studio
cameras, four on microphones and sound, two supplying 'props'
(incidental articles needed for the programme), two shifting scenery, a
Studio Floor Manager, a Director, Production Assistant, Vision
Mixer, Lighting Supervisor, Technical Supervisor, three controlling
the output signals from the cameras, a video-tape machine operator, a
telecine (film) machine operator, three electricians, at least one make-
up artist, and a call boy (for calling performers from their dressing
rooms). In addition, further back behind the scenes, there are film
editors, workshop staff, scenery-builders, wardrobe mistresses, 'props'
curators, secretaries, at least five programme researchers, a
Programme Editor and his deputy. All for 50 minutes of television
each week!

It is the aim of most of these people *never* to be noticed. They are
dedicated to the production of faultless television on the screen.

There must be no wobble on a camera shot. Speech must be clear –
yet no microphone should be seen except, perhaps, in front of a seated
person or held in the hand of a singer. Lights must not cast shadows.
Colour has to be balanced. Film and video-tape recordings should
appear at just the right moment. Programme timings have to be
'counted down' precisely. Performers have to be readied and made-up
in plenty of time.

The production team is usually extremely sensitive to the fact that a
slip-up in their back-room procedures can mar a production just as
easily as the performer forgetting his lines or turning to the wrong
camera.

The Floor Manager

Once the artist has reached the studio, it is actually the job of the
Studio Floor Manager to make sure that everybody is aware of
precisely what is happening. Like the cameraman, he (or she) wears
headphones and is connected to the Control Room, either by wire or
by walkie-talkie. Phrases like 'Stand by for rehearsal' or 'One minute
to transmission' are called out clearly.

It is also the Floor Manager's job to maintain discipline in the
studio and to interpret any frenzied instructions which may be

Floor Manager Pat Greening checks Newcaster's script

shouted, from time to time, by the Director into calm and gentle requests to the performers who may otherwise be upset. Often, considerable tact is called for and most Floor Managers have a strong sense of humour.

In front of the camera

Quite apart from reporters like myself, there are about 200 'front' men and women who appear regularly on British television day after day, week after week. They have one thing in common – they all enjoy their work. The world of television is a friendly world, born partly out of the theatre and partly out of Fleet Street, with all their informalities, demanding discipline only when it matters – in other words, when the studio is 'on air'.

Everybody is on first-name terms. The behind-scenes atmosphere is relaxed for most of the time and there is a great deal of social intercourse. There is also, throughout television, a strong feeling of being part of a team.

Camera, lights, sound, technical facilities and control – these are the basic elements behind every face of the screen. In front, somewhere, sits, stands or lies the viewer. When he is performing in the studio, how conscious is the TV personality of the viewer? Answer: not very.

He is more likely to be thinking of the glint on the camera lens, his script, the voice from the Control Room in his earpiece, a bead of sweat gathering between his eyebrows, the timing signals being indicated on the fingers of the Floor Manager, whether a 'frog' in his

A typical TV studio – Thames TV

throat is going to clear without coughing and last (but not least) if he is going to manage to finish what he is saying just as the production assistant's countdown reaches 'three, two, one, zero, OUT'.

The viewer at the far end is obviously of vital importance – television is for people and not people for television. The letters, the telephoned queries, the criticisms – all these must be answered or taken to heart. But in the long-term, rather than the short-term.

When the camera light goes red, the face on the screen is only really thinking of one person – himself.

Chapter 3
Secrets of the control room

'Let me know when you're ready on the floor.'

Seven men and two women are sitting in semi-darkness, light from a bank of 44 TV monitors blanching their faces and bringing a feverish sparkle to their eyes. Sheets of yellow paper, carefully typed, lie in front of them.

'OK, David, we're ready.'

The disembodied voice from the studio triggers action. The Control Room, where the nine are sitting, is divided into three by glass-panelled sliding doors. To the right are the Sound engineers and technicians; to the left are the Vision and Lighting team; in the centre sits the Director, flanked by his Production Assistant and Vision Mixer – both women on this occasion – and by a Liaison Engineer, who is monitoring signal strengths. It is rehearsal time.

'OK, everybody, going from the top in 15 seconds. Stand by VTR One, this is a rehearsal.'

The Production Assistant reaches forward and presses a blue-tinted button on the console in front of her, marked 'REH'. A translucent panel in the studio lights up with 'REH' and another outside the studio door. Her eyes now are on a clock, about the size of a dinner plate, set in the midst of the TV monitors. Its second hand is jerking.

'Fifteen, fourteen, thirteen,' she begins, 'twelve, eleven, ten . . .'

'Roll VTR One.' As the Director's first 'R' is rolling from his mouth, the Production Assistant presses another button and the hands of the Vision Mixer move to a pair of slim, steel levers which click together to form the 'Master Fader'. It is these, in a few moments, which will bring the picture to the master screen. Meanwhile, one monitor – linked to No 1 Video-Tape-Recorder (VTR 1) in the Central Apparatus Room elsewhere in the building – is beginning to show movement.

'. . . nine, eight, seven, six, five, four, three, two, one . . .'

'Cue "grams". Fade up.' Once again, with only a micro-second of delay, the Director's instructions are translated into action. Music – the programme signature tune – bursts out of the Control Room speakers. The Vision Mixer's hands slide forward and the programme title appears.

'Ten seconds on VTR – coming to Camera One.' The Production

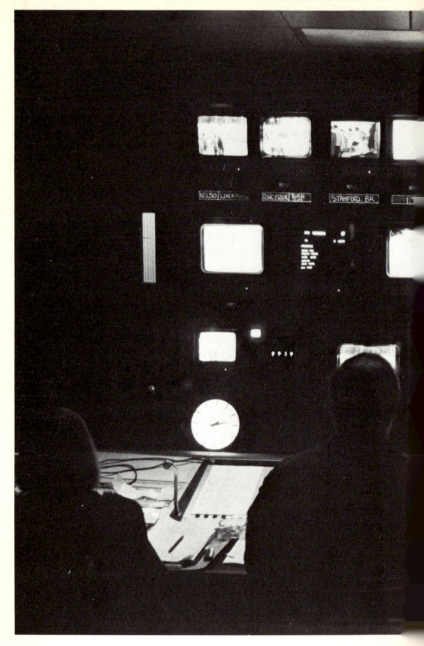

World of Sport *Control Room – London Weekend Television*

Assistant's eyes are on her 'cue-sheet' and stop watch. 'Five, four, three, two, one. . . .'

'Fade "grams". Take One. Cue Gary.'

Another colour monitor leaps to life, this one labelled 'CAM 1'. A red glow appears around its rim, indicating that Camera No. 1 in the studio has gone 'live'. On the screen, the bearded face of Gary, the programme presenter, appears. He begins to speak, reading from the prompting machine.

'Go in a bit closer, One.' The half-figure on the screen enlarges to a head and shoulders as Camera One zooms in slowly.

'Hold it, there's a shadow on his face.' The Lighting Director, in the left-hand Control Room, has noticed it. So, too, has the Sound Supervisor to the right. 'Pull out a bit, Roger,' he orders one of the boom microphone operators. The shadow disappears.

'Right, coming to Telecine 2, we're on Camera One now. Cue Gary again.'

The Production Assistant presses another button marked 'Cue' and Gary continues his opening lines. Just as his script is about to refer to England team manager Don Revie, the Director flicks his fingers and calls 'Take Telecine 2.' A photograph of Don Revie appears, as if by magic, on one of the top line of monitors – slotted into place in a 35mm slide attachment to the No. 2 Telecine (film) projector in the Central Apparatus Room upstairs. Once again, it is the Vision Mixer's quick fingers which switch it on to the screen at just the right moment.

'David, can you talk to me for a moment?' The Floor Manager is calling from the studio. Gary goes burbling on.

'Yes, Pat, what is it?'

'I was worried about my "talkback". It didn't seem to be working.'

'Better check it, Sound.'

The Sound Supervisor moves off his swivel chair and goes personally to the studio, picking up a fresh 'walkie-talkie' with a small whip antenna on the way. The Floor Manager unbelts her faulty one, clips on the fresh one and re-belts it around her slacks. Gary is still burbling.

On the extreme left of the line in the Control Room, the Lighting Console Operator is studying 154 red-and-white squares, each about the size of a postage stamp and each bearing a number. Some are lit, others not. As the rehearsal progresses, new ones light up. They indicate which of the forest of lamps in the studio have gone into action.

'Er, Mike, we should have Rodney Marsh on Telecine 4 – that looks to me like Ian Ball.' Once again, the Director's comment triggers action upstairs in the Apparatus Room, as Mike switches slides in the machine. It is the purpose of rehearsal to correct all such mistakes and to get the 'running order' of supporting visual material into sequence.

'Telecine 3, can I see the first few frames of the golf film from Gleneagles – just the first few secs.?' The Director swivels slightly in his chair, which is made of leather and larger than the rest. He is perspiring. In answer to his request, mouthed down a flexible, chrome-plated microphone, another of the top line of TV monitors flickers with movement.

'Roll Telecine 3.'

The figure 5, encircled in black, in the centre of No. 3 Telecine machine's monitor screen is replaced abruptly by a 4, then a 3, a 2 and a 1. The figures are followed by a sequence of film showing Tony Jacklin putting. The Director waits until the golf ball plops into the hole, then says curtly: 'OK, OK, now punch me up the Manchester OB on Remote One.'

The Vision Mixer's finger plunges. A 'live' view of the crowd at the Manchester United–Newcastle soccer match – transmitted 400 kilometres over telephone lines and microwave links from the Outside Broadcast unit at Manchester – appears on several monitors in each section of the Control Room. All engineers present check it for 'level' – sound level and picture brightness.

'Three minutes to transmission.'

'Right, Gary, let's just rehearse your second intro. Stand by Telecine, 4, Telecine 3 and VTR 1.' Gary shuffles his papers and squares up to the camera again.

'Cue Gary.' The red light goes on. The red glow returns to the rim of the 'CAM 1' monitor. With each reference to a named person, the Director flicks his fingers, the Vision Mixer darts her finger, the picture changes on the screen. It is fast, exacting work and the enemy is time.

'Two minutes to transmission.'

Flickering meter-needles on the Sound console must never 'peak' beyond a certain mark. They have to be watched. Moving wave-forms – like the humps of a sea-serpent – must have the correct contours. They have to be watched on an oscilloscope in front of the Liaison Engineer. Lights must fade up, have the correct colour contrast and dim. They, too, have to be watched.

'OK. Set up for transmission.'

'One minute to transmission.'

Suddenly, there is tension. Fingers shuffle yellow 'cue sheets'. Hands reach for cigarette packs. Eyes carefully scan the monitors for a last pre-view check.

'Forty-five to transmission.'

'Lime juice, please, Bert,' calls Gary, 'and quick.' He faces a four hour marathon. Suddenly his throat is dry. Studio hand Bert whips a pre-mixed glass of cordial from a cabinet, as he has done a hundred times before, and slides forward with it.

'Thanks.' Gary sips, reaches for a mirror and straightens his tie. The make-up girl floats over and dabs his brow with a leather, laced with eau-de-cologne. 'Good luck,' she whispers.

'Thirty seconds.'

Suddenly, the voice of the station Continuity Announcer breaks across the Control Room murmurs. '. . . At eight o' clock we have our thriller – a tale of murder and intrigue set in the Yorkshire Dales – and that's followed at nine by *Within These Walls* starring Googie Withers. But now it's time for . . .'

'Fifteen seconds, fourteen, thirteen, twelve, eleven . . .'

'Roll VTR One.'

'Ten, nine, eight, seven, six, five, four, three, two, one. . . .'

'Go "grams". Fade-up!'

The show has gone 'live'. Millions are now watching. . . .

The identities of the characters in the above script have been deliberately left vague. The scenario and some of the action have been compressed. But the dialogue is fairly typical of that which can be heard in any television Control Room shortly before a programme goes ''on air'. Sometimes rehearsals may take longer – many hours, perhaps, with the action being repeated over and over again so that camera 'shots' can be improved, lights or mikes re-positioned, cuts made in stories, visual back-ups changed. In a full-length drama or fast moving

In 1952, all Britain's TV was monitored from this one panel at the BBC

children's programme, there may be 200 to 300 different camera 'shots', many of them calling for the cameras and their attendant microphones to move about the studio and each 'shot' requiring new lighting.

The Director
All this is the concern of the Director.

The Director may be a man or a woman, and must be quick-thinking, fast-reacting, highly-skilled. Usually, he or she will have come up the hard way – starting, perhaps, as a call-boy or production assistant, advancing to Floor Manager, then on to Vision Mixer – before finally getting a Director's 'ticket'.

World of Sport *Director David Scolt and production team – r. to l. Hilary Deeds (P.A.), Scolt, Daphne Rennie (Vision Mixer), Frank Parker (Engineering Liaison); in background, Sound engineers*

The BBC operates a staff training scheme, with courses lasting for various lengths. A Director's course lasts 2 months. ITV employs a variety of procedures for training and appointing Directors, most of which can be summarised as 'try it and see'.

All vacancies for the post have to be advertised. Candidates go before a selection board, on which sits the Production Controller (who is the Director's immediate boss) and a number of other experts in talent-spotting. They are looking for qualities of commonsense, artistic flair and initiative, which every Director must have, in addition to a thorough background knowledge of technical matters. The chosen person is then usually appointed to the position of 'Trainee Director' and spends anything up to nine months sitting alongside a full Director in the Control Room and then a further year on trial. There is much to be learned.

His responsibilities include camera angles and the framing of 'shots' in the studio, choosing which 'shot' to transmit to the viewer and when, whether to 'mix' from one scene to another or 'wipe' (roll part of the scene away across the screen, as if with a windscreen-wiper), the operation of graphics and animation in the studio, manipulation of slides, film or video-tape from locations both inside and outside the studio, approving the script, approving the clothing and make-up for presenter or actors, rehearsing the team and, finally, taking responsibility for the production going out to the viewer.

The Director is like the captain of a ship, with access to everything, constantly on the alert, responsible if anything goes wrong, in firm command of his crew, friendly with his passengers. The Control Room is his bridge.

Many Control Rooms are actually quite like the bridges of real ships – they look down through large glass windows on what is happening on the studio floor below. Others are more like the Control Room of a submarine – they rely for their information on electronic 'eyes' and 'ears'.

The very latest Control Rooms in British television – completed in June 1973 at London Weekend's complex of studios on the south bank of the river Thames – have no direct view of the studio.

The Control Room attached to Studio 3, for example (which handles *World of Sport*, *Russell Harty Plus*, *Weekend World* and a number of pop shows) relies on 44 monitor screens. The overall impression as you enter is one of soft grey silence. The wall decor is grey, the tops of the consoles are grey, the monitors look grey when 'off air' – only the teak facings to the work-tops, the dark brown carpet tiles and the brightly-coloured switches and buttons relieve the monotony.

The Director sits facing a vertical wall of TV monitors, of varying size, a large loudspeaker with a digital clock above it and another clock with a red second hand. In front of his chair is his console – a 40 centimetre-square steel-grey desk, with a sloping surface to hold notes and cue sheets, 22 silver volume controls and eight coloured switches. Four of these switches (blue, white, yellow and grey) allow him to talk to his camera operators in the studio, three (green, dark blue and white) connect him to Outside Broadcast units and one (red) links him to the London Weekend 'Presentation Area' where sit a Transmission Controller and continuity section, whose job is to ensure that programmes go out on time, that commercials slot in at the right moment, and that no gaps occur.

His 22 volume controls allow him to adjust links with the Studio Floor Manager, Video-Tape-Recording department, Sound Supervisor, Telecine (film playback) department, Central Apparatus Room, Musical Director, Dubbing Theatre, Camera Control, Lighting Supervisor – to name just a few.

He also has 'DIRT' – an acronym for Director's Instant Reverse Talk-In – a cunning switching system which permits him to be in two-way contact with all his Outside Broadcast units (and there may be as many as 12 operating on a Saturday afternoon) simultaneously.

Finally, just to the right of his console, he has a plug to which the *World of Sport* slow-motion replay machine is attached, which he also has to control.

By observing the kaleidoscope of pictures on the TV monitors in front of him, by continuously checking the 'cue-sheets' which supply him with the written outline of the programme, by following his own notes on camera angles and 'shots', the Director cuts the whole programme together electronically by issuing verbal commands, often with a flick of his fingers to ensure exact timings.

His two chief lieutenants are the Production Assistant and Vision Mixer.

The Production Assistant

Production Assistants, or 'PAs', are usually girls. Everyone in television has admiration for them once they are fully trained. They blossom as part-secretary, part-timekeeper, part-public relations expert, part-booking clerk and part-nursemaid. The official 'check-list' issued to trainee PAs in ITV contains 40 different responsibilities.

They are, for example, responsible for the distribution of the script. They must type it and make copies of it. They have to organise the artists – make sure they arrive on time, have dressing rooms, get paid and have meals. The canteen has to be informed. Rail tickets have to be bought, guests met at the station or airport.

They have to order up any 'props' needed for the production and any wardrobe requirements. They also have to make a list of all slides, still photographs, films, video-tapes, sound effects, special effects and discs needed.

They must time every piece of film or video-tape carefully, book recording facilities and book the studio. Once in the Control Room, they are responsible for 'counting down' every recorded item, calling out the time left in a clear voice, so that the Control Room team and artists (through their ear-pieces or with the aid of signals from the Floor Manager) know exactly what point the production has reached.

They have to 'call the shots' – call out to the Director which camera is on, and which is due to go 'live' next. So, throughout a production, you hear this kind of phrase coming from the PA: 'On One, coming to Four' or '15 seconds on VTR, coming to Camera Three'. She gets her guidance from the 'cue sheets' which she has also typed.

Finally, after the show is over, the PA has to note any alterations or variations made on the original script and deposit a copy in the archives.

She is usually first on the scene – and last to leave. A stopwatch becomes her brooch, a pen more important than her purse. Most PAs begin as secretaries or typists within television and then apply to switch to the production side when a vacancy occurs. They have to undergo a minimum of nine months of basic training.

In the Control Room the PA has her own console alongside the Director. In the case of Control Room 3 at London Weekend Television, there are two PA's consoles.

The most interesting of the PA's panoply of controls is the 'cue dot' button. In commercial television, the station transmitting a programme has to indicate to other stations on the network when a commercial break is imminent. This is done by super-imposing a tiny dot of white, or flickering black-and-white, over the picture in the top right-hand corner of the frame. It is usually pulsed out one minute before the commercial break is due. But in a programme such as *World of Sport*, the timing of commercial breaks is flexible.

It is up to the PA to indicate when her Director is about to take a commercial break by using her 'cue dot' button.

The Vision Mixer

The PA, in this particular Control Room, sits on the Director's left. To his right sits the Vision Mixer. The Vision Mixer is basically a magician with pictures. Her instructions will come from the Director in the form of terse commands, such as 'Take One' (switch to Camera One's picture), 'Fade up Two' (bring up Camera Two's picture gradually), 'Fade to black' (make the screen go blank), 'Mix to Two' (mix from the present camera now transmitting to Camera Two's picture) or 'Stand by to Super the caption on Three' (get ready to superimpose the caption being shown by Camera Three over the picture being transmitted).

The Vision Mixer's console for Studio 3 at London Weekend Television has 96 buttons and six levers on one side, and a panel with 41 buttons, five knobs and two joysticks on the other.

Using these, the Vision Mixer can bring any picture on to the air or on to any screen in the Control Room, 'fade' it up or down (brighten it or dim it), 'split' any screen to present more than one picture on it at a time, 'dissolve' from one picture to another (make one gradually disappear while another is superimposed over it) or 'wipe' (literally, wipe the picture – or part of the picture – off the screen as if with a squeegee or windscreen wiper).

'Wiping' is done with the part of the Control Panel set by the Vision Mixer's right hand known as the 'effects bank'. It has a striking array of black-and-white buttons in the upper section, each printed with the design of the pattern to be produced on the screen. 'Wiping' is rather like having an 'electronic stencil' at your disposal. By pushing a button, parts of the picture can be blotted out with any of 32 different silhouettes – rectangles, squares, triangles, diamonds and so forth. The equipment intercepts the electronic signals coming from the camera and juggles with them.

The Vision Mixer selects which effect he or she wants by prodding one of 32 patterned buttons. The silhouette chosen is then positioned over the picture by moving one of two little black joysticks on the control panel – you simply push the joystick in the direction you want it to go, watching how it is behaving on one of the monitor screens. Then you select the colour you want for the effect: this is done by moving the second joystick. It has six possible positions – each marked with the name of a colour (red, magenta, blue, cyan, green, yellow). Finally, there is a 'luminance button' which controls the intensity of the colour.

The 'effects bank' is mainly used in musical productions where attractive picture effects can enhance the singing. It is possible, for example, to make David Essex's head appear in a star-shaped cut-out on the screen.

The Vision Mixer also has nine buttons, set in a square, which allow the 'wiping' to be done from different directions – left to right, right to left, top to bottom, bottom to top, diagonally left or right.

The same little nest of buttons contains some for inlaying captions over a picture, to explain who is speaking or to switch in Chromakey.

Over on the other side of the console, 96 blue, brown or yellow buttons connect to the studio camera circuits, Outside Broadcast circuits and telecine, video-tape or slide machines. One bank of these allows pictures to be 'punched up' on to the preview monitors in the Control Room; another allows the Vision Mixer to experiment with effects and 'set up' a picture before it goes on to the transmission screen; the third is a duplicate used for 'mixing' pictures.

But the real power in the hands of the Vision Mixer lies in a 10-centimetre long lever with a red knob on top known as the 'master fader'. This can fade out any picture to produce a black screen. It is pushed forward at the start of every programme to fade the picture up and pulled back at the end to finish the show.

Those, then, are the Director's personal aides – the Production Assistant and the Vision Mixer. But he is also the head of a much larger technical team, whose skills he must weld together if he is to achieve something memorable for the audience.

Technical Liaison Engineer

Sitting close by him, throughout *World of Sport*, is a Technical Liaison Engineer whose job it is primarily to monitor circuits between the Outside Broadcast units and the Control Room. Anything up to 12 of the 'OB' units may be in action simultaneously, with a signal of varying quality coming from each transmitter. Signals from the 'OB' and the studio have to be synchronised – a procedure known as 'gen-locking'.

For monitoring, the engineer has 72 green buttons on his console, 48 yellow, 12 red, three green and two blue, as well as an oscilloscope.

Sound Engineers

But his controls are child's play compared with those of the Sound Engineers in the glass-panelled room next door. Their array is more like the cockpit of a Jumbo jet. They have literally hundreds of knobs and switches, levers and meters, plugs and sockets to control, in addition to racks of amplifiers, echo-producing equipment, tape and cassette machines, two-way radios and telephone intercoms.

Their eyes are on seven TV monitors and a large 'Peak Programme Meter', whose needle must not jump beyond a certain point, no matter how loud the noise in the studio, or distortion will occur. To control the output of sound during the programme, they have a large red knob – the 'Master Gain Control'.

Any number of microphones may be used during a programme – Hughie Green's *Opportunity Knocks*, for example, has 61 – and each of these has its own circuits and control channels. The myriad controls on the Sound console permit the quality of the sound produced by each mike to be adjusted (known as 'equalising') and loudspeaker or telephone effects to be fed in.

It may be necessary to alter the degree of echo in a studio – perhaps by physically changing the materials in the studio scenery but more usually by processing the sound after it has left the studio.

The kind of echo normally created will depend on the finish of the reflecting surfaces in the studio, their shape and their rigidity. If the surroundings are highly absorbent to sound, the studio will lack reverberation and seem 'dead': only the direct sound will be heard. If they are shiny and reflective, some of the frequencies in the sound may be

A Sound Supervisor's panel

re-inforced, making the sound 'hard', 'hollow' or 'woofy'. If the reflecting surface is hanging unsupported, the material is liable to resonate. If very hard reflecting surfaces are set so far away from the source of the sound that a delay of more than one eighteenth of a second occurs, between direct pick-up of the sound and the pick-up of its reflection, then the echo which results may be confusing and make the sound unintelligible.

All these factors have to be taken into account by the Sound Supervisor, who can make adjustments in a number of ways. He can adjust volume by altering his amplifier or the position of the microphone. By selecting the correct mike and placing it carefully, he can adjust the proportion of direct sound picked up compared with reflected sound. He can change the tonal quality of the sound by deliberately boosting or cutting off certain frequencies in it inside his electronic equipment. Finally, with recorded sound, he can play around with its pitch and duration, reverse it, repeat it over and over again, or add synthetic noises to it.

Devices known as compressors control the loudness of the sound, while limiters prevent sudden noises from becoming distorted: for example, a weak voice can be made to sound firm, extra 'punch' can be given to the voice used in a commercial, or the blare of a pop group can be toned down by twiddling the knobs on the console.

Ten blue-grey knobs control sound going back into the studio – known as 'foldback'. This is apparently essential to modern pop groups – they expect to hear their own sounds played back to them. I was told: 'It makes them feel they're good. It's like singing in the bath.'

Vision Control and Lighting Engineers

On the opposite side of the Control Room – again separated by a wall of windows – are the Vision Control and Lighting engineers. They have three consoles, three swivel chairs.

Chair No. 1 is occupied by the Vision Controller. He sets the technical quality for all pictures leaving the cameras in the studio. He has eight small toggles for correcting the colour balance – giving more or less intensity of red, green or blue – four iris controls (the camera iris can be opened or closed a little, depending on the brightness of the studio lighting), four black speaker switches and an oscilloscope.

He also has 48 bright yellow buttons which not only allow him to preview the camera 'shots', by bringing them into view on any of 11 monitor screens in the front of his Control Room, but also allow him to give each cameraman a view of what *another* camera is showing. As I explained in Chapter 2, at the back of each camera in the studio is a viewfinder which is like a miniature TV set in itself. The Vision

Close-up of Lighting Console, Studio 3 LWT – buttons on left insert lighting 'plot' into a computer; small squares at top indicate which lights are on in studio

Controller can switch any other camera's picture on to that viewfinder at any time, to give the operator an idea, before he goes 'live', of what kind of 'shot' the preceding camera has been showing. He may then 'frame' his own to match it.

The strength and form of signals leaving each camera varies. These variations are known as 'waveforms' – they have the shapes of ocean waves when fed into an oscilloscope, which shows them up as patterns on a screen. The heights and distances between the peaks of the waves are checked by the Vision Controller, from time to time, on the small oscilloscope in front of him.

Next to the Vision Controller sits the Lighting Director. He is responsible for all the lights in the studio – in the case of Studios 1 and 2 at London Weekend Television, 256 lights; in the case of Studio 3, 128 lights. Not all these lights will be needed for every production and, when a programme is planned, the Lighting Director draws up a 'plot'. This looks like a chart, ruled off in small squares, on which are drawn the different camera and performer positions and movements. The Lighting Director then marks in, in red crayon, which lights will be needed to illuminate the scenes to best advantage.

He can then actually 'store' the sequence of instructions to these lights – the switch on or off, brightening or dimming signals – in a simple computer which stands in the Control Room behind him. As the production progresses, so the various combinations of lights will automatically spring into action. He can store up to 99 'plots' at a time in the machine.

To set all this up, the Lighting Director has his own Console Operator, who sits in the last of the chairs in the Control Room. Whereas the senior man's desk seems relatively uncluttered – a mere 24 buttons (linked to the preview monitors), eight knobs and an inter-com – the Operator's is formidably complex.

For a start, there is a red-and-white translucent indicator light for every light in the studio. If the white half is illuminated, it means the light is on in the studio; if the red part is glowing, it means the light is standing by in some 'plot' lodged in the computer.

Then there is the little keyboard of grey buttons numbered 0 to 9 by which the operator communicates with the computer – tapping in the number of each light in turn as he sets up the 'plot' – and 20 illuminated buttons showing what he has tapped in.

Next, there are the Channel Selector levers – four of them, marked A, B, C and D – by which the operator puts banks of lights into action. Two of these channels may be required when making up the 'plot', the other two are available for 'live' transmissions.

Finally, there are eight more levers – four with black knobs, four with red – which are the 'faders'. They allow lamps to be dimmed or brightened to order: black levers control 'cross-fading' from one lamp to another, red levers control whole 'plots' (a red lever, for example, would be used to switch from a day scene to a night scene). Lighting is a complex art which demands a sharp eye for detail.

The Lighting Director has to consider the angle of the light, the area it will cover, its intensity, how 'hard' or 'soft' it should be and whether it should be white light or coloured. 'Hard' light is easily localised but produces shadows. 'Soft' light will not produce shadows – and may even soften shadows produced by 'hard' lights – but it is less easily localised. The Lighting Director usually prepares a 'plot' which con-tains a blend of both.

He has to be careful about surfaces: shiny surfaces may reflect his lights and the reflections may be seen by the camera. He may also have to be careful about the faces due to appear on the screen – human faces are rarely symmetrical and, if he does not check, he may em-phasise some irregularity with his lights.

It is not surprising, therefore, that lighting is a lengthy process. It is usually scheduled to accompany 'setting' – placing the scenery, placing any 'props' and marking out camera, microphone and performers' positions. Commonly it takes a full day, perhaps from 8am to 9pm, to prepare the studio for a major production.

The Control Room, then, is occupied by the second echelon of the army of people who bring TV to our screen, who maintain continuous contact with the 'front' men in the studio via their ear-pieces or through the medium of the Floor Manager's hand signals.

In the Control Room, you can see and hear virtually everything which is happening in the studio – a fact which performers often forget. I remember very clearly an incident on 20 November 1969 when the Queen officially opened the new studios of ITN in Wells Street, London.

It was Moon-walking time. Alan Shepard and Alan Bean had been out on the Moon that day and the whole studio had been converted into an Apollo 'set' with sand-tables, models and a fully-suited 'astronaut' incorporated in the display. Alastair Burnett, Paul Haney and I – the three 'front' men for the Apollo 12 programme – were to meet the Queen. David Nicholas, producer of the Apollo 'specials', was to present her with a model of a Lunar Module as a souvenir from the ITN Space Unit.

But we were all desperately tired. I had been up most of the night studying the Mission Plan of the astronauts and working out visual tricks by which the studio could compensate for the fact that Alan Bean had hit the lunar camera on the head with a hammer, thus blotting out all TV from the Moon. We had also completed a five-hour 'on air' marathon.

After the Queen had unveiled the plaque, shaken our hands, discussed the use of the sand-table, accepted our gift and left the studio, I sank into a chair, put my feet up on the desk and told the Floor Manager 'Wake me up on lift-off' – in other words, in 10 minutes time when the news bulletin was due to begin. I then, apparently, snored.

When the news was over, ITN gave the Queen a party. I happened to be standing near the door when she entered and she came up to me and said 'Mr Fairley, how do you do it?' A bit perplexed, I asked, 'Do what, ma'am?'

'Go to sleep just before a bulletin.'

I suddenly realised that she had watched me snoring from the Control Room: not just on one monitor, I was told later, but on a dozen.

I tried to explain that television teaches you to switch off parts of your brain, more or less at will, in order to blot out unwanted stimuli and that I had learned to catnap. Because she seemed so very natural and friendly, I asked a question in return.

'How is it, ma'am,' I said, 'that *you* are the only person who has ever been allowed to start the news late?' (There had been a delay of 10 seconds at the start of the transmission.)

'I'm glad you asked that,' she replied, 'I wondered about that too.

Author shows the Queen ITN's models used in coverage of Apollo 12 moon mission

But there were so many other fingers trying to do it for me – you would think that, with all the experience of pushing buttons that I've had, they'd have trusted me!'

Master Control

Normally, the moment of transmission is not controlled by a switch in the Studio Control Room but from elsewhere – usually the 'Presentation Area'. In there sits the station presenter (often called the 'link man' because he links programmes together with a few words) the Transmission Controller and a highly-responsible engineer.

Master Control, as the title suggests, has overall responsibility for the levels of picture and sound leaving the station and for the quality of the 'sync pulses' (signals to mark the end of each 'line' in the 405 or 625-line picture being transmitted from the station which enable electron 'guns' in the home TV sets to be synchronised. More will be said about these very important signals in Chapter 5.)

Each Master Control Room is different. Some Controllers actually switch inputs of signals from studios, video-tape playback machines and telecine machines themselves: others merely act in a supervisory capacity.

In some companies, Master Control is responsible for ensuring that the station's various outputs are combined into one complete, smooth presentation for the viewer. He sees that the station identification symbol and theme-tune, commercial advertisements, trailers for future programmes, apology captions and presenter's 'links' are inserted into the correct slots in the day's programming, without any noticeable pauses. It is through him also, that incoming recordings are fed to the appropriate departments.

During transmission of a play, film, documentary, children's or current affairs programme, the Controller is usually passive, calmly checking signal levels (which have probably already been checked). But during a station break or with Outside Broadcast units in action, he may have to work frenziedly to complete all the necessary switching operations. Such times are referred to, jokingly, as 'panic periods'. The correct picture and sound sources have to be switched 'on air' at the right moment: telecine and video-tape machines may also have to be started 'on cue'.

There is a tendency towards automation in Master Control these days because timings are usually pre-determined. Commercial advertisements are either seven seconds, 15 seconds, 30 seconds, 45 seconds or one minute in length and 'slots' must not exceed three and a half minutes. The time allotted for station identification and programme trailers is also usually fixed well in advance. For this reason, it is difficult to describe a 'typical' Master Control Room and its equip-

Master Control, Thames Television, Teddington

ment because some contain a high degree of automation and others do not.

But probably the most snug is at Thames Television's studios near Teddington.

The Controller there sits in a comfortable chair facing a compact bank of five monitor screens, mounted on a pillar.

The arms of his chair have two in-built panels of finger-tip controls called 'matrixes' – multicoloured switches, buttons and knobs which allow the Controller to bring up any picture or sound so that he can pre-view it before 'cutting to line' (sending it to the transmitter).

There are two 'lines' – circuits linking the studios at Teddington to the ITV network. Each has its own console, set in a curved array to the left and right of him, together with wedge-shaped panels of sound controls. At the end of each array is an oscilloscope on which the Controller can observe the waveform of the signals going to the transmitter.

In another part of the room is a machine with slots for 'spotmasters' – cartridges on which station announcements or short commentaries can be recorded. To load these, he has to leave his chair, but, having loaded them, he can activate them from the comfort of his seat, once more, by pressing one of the matrix of buttons on the arms.

Pictures and sound from Teddington are fed to Thames Television's headquarters in Euston Road, London where another Master Controller relays them to the IBA's transmitter at West Norwood. A fraction of a second later, they are received by millions of people in their homes.

The pictures seen on television, as I have indicated earlier, come from five basic sources: from a studio, from an Outside Broadcast unit, from film, from slides or from video-tape. All these can be switched 'on air' from the Control Room or, in the case of the BBC, from the Central Apparatus Room.

The BBC's Central Apparatus Room is located on the third floor of Television Centre and occupies some 1200 square metres of floor space. It contains banks of monitors, pulse generators, test equipment, synchronising equipment and switching gear for both vision and sound. It is really the technical nerve centre for both BBC networks and is linked to two presentation rooms – known as Network 1 and Network 2 – where announcers link the programmes together. These may be 'live' or recorded on video-tape or film.

Telecine

About 50 per cent of all the visual material seen on television originates as film although this percentage is likely to diminish as video-tape recording equipment becomes more flexible. The TV industry sprang, to a considerable degree, out of the motion picture industry and it is

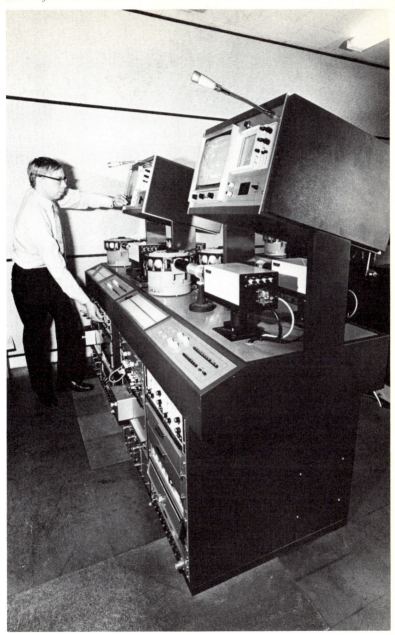

Telecine Slide Scanners – slide is placed in drum for scanning and converting into TV picture

not surprising, therefore, that film techniques and equipment are still widely used throughout television.

Film cameras are relatively simple and portable. Film has, until recently, been comparatively cheap, although processing is expensive. The machines which play back films on television are called 'telecine machines' or 'film scanners'. One type of telecine machine consists, essentially, of a TV pick-up camera looking straight into the lens of a conventional film projector. The TV camera scans each frame of film as it is held stationary for a tiny fraction of a second.

A second type, called a 'flying spot telecine', contains a cathode-ray tube which shines light through the film and scans it converting the pattern of light which gets through into a pattern of voltages by means of a photo-electric cell. It is really like a TV camera in reverse.

In colour TV, the light which passes through the film is analysed into its red, green and blue components. Each component produces its own electrical signal. The three voltage waveforms which emerge represent the intensity of the original colours on the film and are turned into one TV signal for transmission and reproduction on the receiver at home.

Films run at a standard projection rate of 24 frames a second, television produces 25 complete frames a second. Happily, it is possible to reproduce films on TV without any detectable speed-up. The original film may be either 8mm, 16mm or 35mm but only the last two are considered to give high-quality reproduction on TV.

Amateur cine enthusiasts generally use 8mm film, rather than wider varieties because an 8mm camera is smaller, lighter and cheaper. As a result, much of the film reaching ITN or BBC News from amateur sources requires special treatment as well as a special projector. It is sometimes the *only* film available of a news incident, however, and is usually acceptable for the news value of such film far outweighs its technical imperfections. But other films – feature films, movies or sequences shot by TV film crews – must be of good quality in order not to irritate the viewer. Densely opaque prints, 'flat' prints or prints containing extremes of contrast are avoided, if possible.

Film editors are very chary of using the original negative of a film – for fear of damaging it – but prefer, instead, to work with positive prints. They may make two or three, for editing purposes, before the film goes to the telecine machine for transmission. Before the film enters the machine, it is always given a 'leader' – a strip of film containing some blank frames for winding round the spool and frames containing the title and number of the film (to help identification). Sometimes about 100 extra frames are included to allow the telecine machine to get up speed before the picture actually appears. It is this last set which enables the telecine operator to position the film precisely in the machine, so that when the Director in the Control

Film Editor prepares to cut news film

Room·says 'Roll Telecine', the film appears on screen at just the right moment.

Many telecine machines today are started by remote control, requiring no projectionist once they have been loaded. But a telecine operator is still necessary because the machine's controls have constantly to be adjusted in order to get the best results.

Really old film from official archives – such as that now stored in the Imperial War Museum – requires extra-careful handling because the material used in the print is highly inflammable. Even when the film is merely being run through a special projector, a technician has to stand by with a fire extinguisher at the ready.

On one occasion in 1965 – actually the first night Gordon Honeycombe read the ITN news – the telecine equipment itself caught fire. The fire broke out exactly 20 minutes after some witches in the Isle of Man had given a warning of dire consequences if ITN decided not to screen a film showing their coven performing a ritual! One of the witches had rung up to check if the story – filmed the previous day by an ITN cameraman who happened to be passing by – would be used that night as promised. On being told that it would not (it had been decided to scrap it on grounds of public taste, because the witches were naked) she had screamed down the telephone 'You'll be sorry.'

No one was sorrier than Gordon Honeycombe, who had an anxious time wondering whether visual material would appear on the screen to back up his words. Somehow, it did.

Slides

Modern telecines are often 'multiplexed' – linked together – to handle a variety of visual inputs. A 'multiplex' might contain one 35mm projector, one 16mm projector and one slide projector, with the scanning done by three colour vidicon camera tubes. The magazines for the slide projectors can be loaded with transparencies in advance and these can then be fed, by remote control, into the machine. This system is used every night for news bulletins.

Each slide has to be placed carefully so that it is the right way up, the right way round and in the right position in the running order. Telecine preview monitors in the Control Room enable the Director to check these things before the slide is shown 'on air'.

It was a 35mm colour slide which, in 1973, gave me my worst moment in television. It was during the second mission involving Skylab, the orbital space station, when a crew of American astronauts had been living inside for more than a month. The mission commander was Alan Bean, whose home I had visited some time previously in Houston. Sue Bean, Alan's wife, had just arrived in London for a holiday with their two children, Clay and Sue.

Because of limitations on space at the back of the Control Room, it was only possible to take the two Bean children into the Control Room to see the 5.50pm news bulletin transmitted: the others had to watch it on monitors in the Green Room.

It so happened that an item about Skylab was scheduled for that particular news bulletin – Alan Bean and his crew had set up a new space endurance record. I remember leaning, slightly smug, against a pillar in the Control Room with the astronaut's children beside me when Sue Bean said suddenly, 'Why has Pete Conrad's crew appeared on that screen?'

Sure enough, the faces of astronauts Pete Conrad, Joe Kerwin and Paul Weitz – who had carried out the *first* mission to Skylab – had come up on one of the telecine preview monitors. 'I don't know,' I told Sue. 'I'll find out.' I slid forward and asked the Director. 'The second Skylab crew have set up a new endurance record,' he replied. 'Yes,' I said, *'but you've got the wrong crew on the slide.'*

I have never moved so fast – down a corridor and up two flights of stairs to the News Information department, where the 35mm colour slides are kept. 'Quick,' I gasped, 'give me a slide of Alan Bean, Owen Garriott and Jack Lousma.' The girl reacted swiftly. Seconds later, I was in the Central Apparatus Room nearby, watching a telecine operator switch the slides.

We made it with five seconds to spare.

Video-tape

The Central Apparatus Room at ITN has 'multiplexes' and contains four telecine machines for film, three for scanning slides, two caption-scanners and seven video-tape machines. Video-tape is a direct alternative to film.

Video-tape recording (VTR)

A video-tape recording (VTR) apparatus accepts signals direct from a TV camera, or from the vidicon tubes of telecine machines, and stores them on magnetic tape – in much the same way as an audio tape recorder accepts sounds, except that the tape is much wider.

Whereas the audio tape-recorder registers the spectrum of sound converted into electrical impulses by a microphone and amplifier, the VTR machine registers the visual spectrum converted into electrical signals from a TV source. But the range of the frequencies which have to be recorded from television makes the VTR machine a more complicated and much larger piece of apparatus – almost as large as a double wardrobe in a bedroom.

The advantages of using VTR – as opposed to film or tele-recording (a method of transferring television directly onto film, using a special camera) – are that the pictures can be played back instantly, need no processing in a laboratory and can be edited without cutting. They can also be erased, so that the tape can be used over and over again (in the case of today's colour tapes, from 75 to 100 times).

Present-day VTR machines have a facility which allows the recorded pictures to be edited electronically without cutting and splicing the tape. Magnetic pulses – known as 'edit pulses' – are recorded on the control track running along the side of the tape all the time and these indicate the boundaries between one picture and the next. When a sequence of VTR has to be edited, one of these pulses is located as the starting point and another as the finishing point and the whole sequence is then transferred to another machine. All the operator has to do is to press a button where he wants the editing to begin. He can rehearse the edit as often as he wishes – another advantage over film.

Many people in the television industry are convinced that this facility is the key to faster, less expensive programme-making in the future. By taking a TV camera onto location, recording the signals directly onto VTR and then editing electronically, it is possible not only to complete a high-quality programme quickly but avoid the need for film developing and cutting, which is becoming increasingly expensive. Furthermore, the tape can be 'wiped' afterwards and used again.

Chapter 4
The backroom boys – and girls

Props

A telephone rings in the room at the top. A voice says, 'We want a pillar box, a barrel organ, a bust of a Greek god, five large balloons and a rubber tree.' Mentally, the man answering the telephone ticks them off. 'You can have them all except the barrel organ,' he replies. 'I'll have to try to borrow that. I think I know a vicar who collects them.'

Bill Smith reaches for his coat.

One hundred and sixty kilometres away in Manchester, Spud Taylor is looking at a document headed 'Requirements'. It lists a five-ton Bedford lorry, two Bren guns on tripods, 12 rifles with bayonets, an early Polish mine-detector, 45 metres of signal cable, some khaki pyjamas, a German officer's revolver with holster, a Penguin paperback called *Death of a Hero*, a Thompson sub-machine gun and 48 bottles of Stella lager.

Over the water in Ulster, John Floyd is coping with a request for a bottomless bath. Up in Carlisle, Harry King is scouring the town for an old Austin Seven car – to paint in psychedelic colours. Down in Cardiff, Dorothy Dawe is contacting animal trainers to find a barking alligator.

Bill Smith, Spud Taylor, John Floyd, Harry King and Dorothy Dawe have one thing in common. They are in the properties business – not land or housing but *objects*: objects required in TV productions. Their job is to find them, hire them, buy them or have them made, no matter how bizarre the object requested.

The 'props' people, as they are known, form part of the third echelon in the army of men and women involved in bringing TV to the screen – backroom boys and girls who work, literally, behind the scenes.

Like the scenery builders themselves, the special effects men, the graphics artists, the make-up girls, the programme researchers and the wardrobe mistresses, they face a fresh set of challenges with every programme. Their work may take hours, yet what they achieve may be in vision for only a matter of seconds.

'Props' people have a universal motto: 'The impossible takes a little longer.' Their store-rooms range in size from a pantechnicon to an aircraft hangar. Walk around them and you may see a Paris newspaper kiosk leaning drunkenly against the remains of a Wild West

saloon, a bamboo bar littered with swordsticks and umbrellas, por-
traits of Lord Nelson and Charles the Second alongside those of Adolf
Hitler and the Czar Nicholas, notices in 20 different languages, chan-
delier lamps, ashtrays, busts, telephone boxes, brass statues of
Buddha, rifles and artificial flowers.

Any new TV series, especially if set in a particular period in history,
may pose a thousand headaches for the 'props' department.

To help them make a series authentic, they usually work hand-in-
glove with the Programme Researchers.

Programme Researchers

Programme Researchers, someone once said, need to know *everything*.
They need to know where to get the facts and how to extract the facts.
They have to be patient, curious, persistent, accurate, tactful and
determined not to be beaten. They must learn to deal in minutiae,
gather their information quickly and assemble it in a form palatable to
the user.

Many TV researchers have had experience on newspapers and arrive
with some expertise in interviewing, fact-assembling and summarising,
as well as with their own list of contacts. Others start from scratch –
often straight from university.

Sometimes the researcher has to travel thousands of kilometres and
telephone people all over the world to obtain what is needed.

Margaret Lord, one of Granada's senior researchers, tells the story
of how she located beer labels for a scene set in a Cairo pub in 1943.
The script called for the hero to be drinking beer on leave from the
desert fighting. The beer in Egypt at that time was 'Stella'. 'I rang
round all the brewers in Britain,' explains Margaret, 'but nobody had
heard of the stuff. In the end, I contacted the military attaché at the
Egyptian Embassy in London. A few days later, he rang back with the
name of a firm in Cairo. I then telephoned Cairo. The firm sent me
some labels which we copied and stuck on bottles of the right shape.
They looked just right.'

Margaret adds: 'It's quite usual to go to that amount of trouble. But
I must say that, when it came to filming, I kept wanting to rush on and
turn all the bottles round so that the viewer could see my labels!'

Research for a programme such as Thames Television's *This Is Your
Life* may call for the researcher to spend a day with a Hollywood film
star in the Dorchester Hotel or a week living with a family in a slum in
Glasgow, interviewing relatives of the boy who 'made good'.

The Set Designer

The 'set' (full name 'setting') itself is another of the Director's responsibilities and, in a major production, he will call in a Set Designer.

It may be a farmhouse kitchen, the bridge of a warship, an elegant

Kensington drawing room or a swinging discothèque – whatever the scene, it is the Set Designer's job to visualise it in three dimensions and transpose it from the drawing board to the studio. Unlike theatre or films, TV calls for sets which can be seen from many angles. The Set Designer has to take into account the movement and positioning of cameras, microphones and lighting. He also has to have a good knowledge of materials (their reflective and sound-dampening characteristics and structural properties) of architecture, furniture and costume.

A TV set under construction

He usually begins by preparing two studio plans to a scale of quarter-inch-to-one-foot on squared paper – one gives a bird's eye view of the set, the other a side view. After these have been approved, copies go to the Director, Lighting Director, Scenery Department and 'Props'. Sometimes a scale model is built.

The set is frequently the most expensive part of a TV production. The series *Edward the Seventh* called for a particular room in Windsor Castle to be copied in the studio, down to the smallest stick of furniture in it. Cost: around £8,000. For the series *Clayhanger*, set in the Potteries, an entire street was reconstructed at Elstree Studios. Price: about £45,000. And for the February 1976 production of *Peter Pan*, which starred Danny Kaye as Captain Hook and Mia Farrow as Peter, ATV built a reproduction of half a pirate ship 20 metres long, 15 metres wide, with a poop deck, quarter deck, lower deck and gun deck, complete with 11 cannons. Price: more than £10,000. The pirate ship was built on scaffolding, mounted on castors, and more than 1,300 metres of rope went into the rigging, which had to support Mia Farrow.

The scenery builders

The actual job of constructing the set is done by a platoon of carpenters, metal-workers, painters and handymen in the Scenery Building Department. This is, physically, the largest department in most TV studios.

The BBC's Scenery Department at Shepherd's Bush covers nearly half a hectare. Once the scenery and 'props' have been made they are moved onto a runway which has direct access to all seven production studios or to vans which carry pieces to regional studios. Some 8,000 individual 'sets' and 370 backcloths are completed each year and there is storage space for 5,000 pieces of furniture and 15,000 'props' of assorted sizes.

Sets are usually built from a number of separate, pre-fabricated units which are positioned and then fastened together. Sometimes they are 'dressed' afterwards with drapes or furnishings to give a total scenic effect. Many of the components are designed so that they can be used over and over again. They have technical names like 'flats', 'solid pieces', 'cut-outs' and 'backgrounds'.

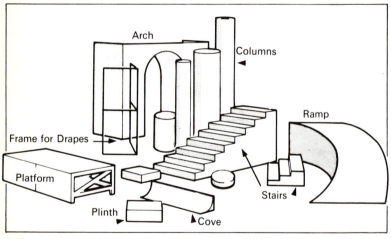

Different types of scenery

'Flats' are wooden frames, ranging in size from two metres to five metres high and two centimetres to four metres wide, faced either with hardboard, plywood or fireproofed hessian. They are nailed or hinged together.

The surfaces of 'flats' can be treated in a variety of ways – with paint or distemper, wallpaper, papier mâché or patterned fabric, or even with a facing of wire mesh.

'Solid pieces' fall into two categories – architectural imitations and structural supports.

Architectural units include such things as doorways, fire-places, windows, staircases, balconies; columns and lamp-posts. They are usually built as hollow, wooden shells which can either stand free or be 'plugged' into apertures in 'flats'. Structural supports are usually more rigid and include steps and blocks which may either raise the height of other pieces of scenery or allow the actors to move onto different levels.

'Cut-outs' (also sometimes called 'profile pieces') are fashioned out of plywood, hardboard or compressed card and attached to supporting blocks before being painted. They are frequently used to give 'depth' to a scene and are comparatively cheap to make.

'Backgrounds' may be solid or fabric, painted or projected. They may be formed out of 'flats' linked together; out of 'drapes' of cotton, wool or velvet; out of 'backcloth' – canvas or twill, usually hung from a pole or fastened to battens; or out of screens, onto which film or photographic effects can be projected or 'inlaid'. They may be in neutral colours and have a smooth finish or be textured in a number of different ways.

The painter can simulate mouldings, brickwork or panelling with his brush alone. Or the scenery-builder may use photographic wallpapers or wooden sheets to give extra realism, especially if the surface is likely to be seen in close-up.

Scenery being painted, Teddington studios

Plastics, fibre-glass, plaster and papier mâché – all these can be transformed into realistic objects by the TV craftsmen. Tree-trunks, cobblestones, brick walls, fountains, statues – each calls for its own material, depending on how durable it has to be and how closely the camera will view it.

The studio floor itself may have to be painted. Generally speaking, studio floors are in neutral colours but they can be given water-paint treatment to suggest floor-boards, paving stones or carpets. Sometimes sawdust, cork or peat is scattered for effect – but never salt or sand, for these can ruin valuable studio equipment. When more substantial floor coverings are called for – such as carpets, tarpaulins or even turf – care has to be taken to see that the cameras and micro-phones can still move around freely on their 'dollies'.

Gauzes are used widely in TV scenery. They may be stretched across windows instead of glass to suggest a perspective beyond, laid over background scenery to soften textures or contrasts, or hung with attachments to suggest objects floating in space.

The Cyclorama, or 'cyc', may be made out of gauze, duck-cloth, canvas or velour, as alternatives to plywood or hardboard. The shallow, C-shaped surface can be tinted with a mid-grey finish to make a neutral background for almost any scene in the studio, or lit in various ways to suggest shadows, sky or space. Small 'cycs' are sometimes fixed as backings to windows.

The scenery builder has a number of other tricks for simulating objects which are either too large, heavy or inconvenient, in real life, to be transported into the studio. Glass, for example, may get accidentally smashed – so plastic, gauze or tracing linen may be used instead. 'Sugar-glass' (made out of sugar melted in troughs to give large see-through panels) or brittle plastic are used if the glass has to be smashed as part of the plot. Frost patterns can be mimicked by stippling glass with a mixture of stale beer and Epsom salts.

Rocks, boulders or caves can be created out of wood and wire mesh, with canvas, papier mâché, or plaster moulded on to the framework. Gravel – which sounds excessively noisy inside a studio – is often simulated with fine cork chips, whilst dust and dirt are usually replaced by coloured sawdust or Fuller's earth.

Water is sometimes 'made' out of plate glass laid on top of black velvet: studio lights can create a ripple effect. A 'wet look' to other surfaces may be achieved by spraying them with glycerine, varnish or a soluble glue. Ice can be cellophane or a sheet of glass laid on a light coloured cloth.

To give a 'lived-in' look to some settings, a process known as 'antiqueing', 'blowing down' or 'dirtying-up' is used. This involves spraying a fine film of dark water-paint around door frames, in crevices, at the edges of pictures and by light-switches and door handles. Peeling paper can be simulated by tearing the paper and then holding it back against the wall with invisible threads: releasing these causes the paper to peel.

On location

Many such elaborate tricks can, of course, be avoided if the cameras, actors and production team all move into real surroundings – on location. Obviously, it depends on two factors – cost, and whether a suitable location can be found.

On location

To find the right place, producers often use location agencies. Bill Moxey started one in 1968, Camera Location Services. Today he is able to offer TV and film companies a heterogeneous selection of locations including riverside warehouses, baronial manors, gazebos, thatched cottages, bandstands, churches, judges' chambers, Mayfair flats, orangeries, terraces of Victorian houses, an operating theatre, mortuary – even a lighthouse.

Bill can provide a Mediterranean-type scene within five kilometres of Piccadilly Circus, a waterfall near London, or an almond tree blossoming out of season, deserted beaches, main roads with white lines down the middle but no traffic, a house waiting to be demolished, a submarine, 145 kilometres of private railway or a 200 year old dungeon.

Anne Glanfield runs a firm called Locations Unlimited. She keeps 20,000 photographs. 'Sometimes,' she says, 'producers want a stately home or something very unlikely like a penthouse flat with a sunken bath, but 60 per cent of the time they want ordinary houses. We're always looking for attractive lounges, bedrooms, kitchens, bathrooms and gardens.'

Anne – who found most of the locations for the police series *The Sweeney* – rates as her most difficult assignment the task of arranging for comedian Barry MacKenzie to go down London's sewers in a boat!

Usually, TV directors come to her with a script. 'We then go through it to see what is needed,' she explained, 'and we do a location breakdown. We go through our files, get out the pictures and the director chooses. Then he usually does a personal recce. But our part saves him a lot of time.'

Fees negotiated by Anne range from £75 a day for a suburban semi-d. to £500 a day for a stately home. 'The point about the stately home is that it often saves the director the expense of hiring "props" – they're all in there from the start. As far as a housewife in a semi-d. is concerned, £75 may seem a lot of money. But when a TV crew moves in, it really is a circus. It's chaos, even though the company employs someone to sweep up all the mess afterwards. There are usually about 25 people, plus generators, cables and a catering van. *Very* disruptive.'

Special effects

Snow falling thick enough to show a perfect footprint, rain drizzling or splattering down like a monsoon, bullets ricocheting off rocks, a knife thrust into a man's chest, arrows piercing the heart, blood spurting – all are 'props' devised by the special effects men, most of whom have a thorough knowledge of mechanical engineering and chemistry as well as other qualifications.

Les Dowie, special-effects expert, once used enough high explosive in an episode of *Manhunt* to reduce the Houses of Parliament to rubble – *and* 5,000 litres of petrol to feed the flames!

He and his team have made the moon – and created the world – more times than they care to remember. 'My favourite ingredient for creating a world is simmering porridge,' he explains. 'It slurps and bubbles marvellously, and it looks great when filmed.'

Destruction and unlikely methods of inflicting sudden death are, however, his main occupation. He has planned hundreds of aircraft crashes and has written-off more than 50 cars. 'It's not always easy to arrange for a car to burst into flames at just the right moment when it's tumbling halfway down a cliff,' he admits.

One of the most enjoyable days I have ever spent was with Roland Chenakee, head of the special effects department at Universal Studios in Hollywood. First he revealed to me the secrets of *Six Million Dollar Man*. 'It's mostly wire-work. We fit a harness to him with two thin wires running 30 metres up to a crane above. Every time he takes giant strides or vaults a fence, we simply crank him up. The wires don't show. We use the same technique when he picks up cars – the cars are wired. We also use a special, high-speed camera to film him. When the film is played back, he appears to be moving in slow motion all the time.'

Lee Majors, who played the title role, had a habit of getting into the middle of explosions – but always escaping from them. No surprise. The flames were real, but the material used was flaked naphthalene which produced the minimum of heat.

Next, the secrets of the westerns. Every time a cowboy is hurled through a 'glass' window, he shuts his eyes just before striking the pane. This is to avoid splinters. For the 'glass' – which used to be made out of sugar – is now made out of a plastic called C-2 which shatters realistically but produces fine splinters. Window-frames are made of balsa wood and painted to look solid.

None of the fighters' punches connect, except those to the stomach. 'The guy on the receiving end just has to tense his midriff muscles and take it as best he can. He has to be pretty fit.'

A simple gunfight may take a fortnight to 'block-out' – practice the movements and actions – before the filming begins. A whipping may take three or four days of rehearsal: whips never touch, but the aim has to be accurate for the end of the whip is travelling at around 125 kilometres per hour and could easily produce a gash one centimetre deep in the flesh, were it to touch accidentally.

'Have a look at this,' he went on, handing me a body-belt faced with a line of small, plastic sachets. 'It's our latest thing for cowboys, cops and hoodlums.' Each sachet contained a sweet-smelling red substance which glistened in the light.

Body-belts like it are part of the secret of the realism in police series such as *The Streets of San Francisco*, or *McCloud*.

'In the days of black-and-white movies, we had to make our "blood" out of chocolate syrup – anything red would come out on film as grey. But now, with colour, we use either Max Factor "Panchromatic Blood", which is fairly dark, or a mixture of water, cochineal food colouring and glycerine. The glycerine keeps it glossy under the lights.' Three methods of releasing the imitation blood are used – the good old 'You've got me' method where the actor slaps his wound and breaks open the bag, allowing the blood to seep through his clothing; or where one actor shoots another with a gun loaded with blood; or the new body-belt method.

The belt itself is leather. Discs of lead are embedded in it, each capped by a tiny explosive charge. The sachets of blood are fastened over the caps which are linked (by thin wires) electrically to a firing mechanism resembling a typewriter. When the actor is shot, a studio technician 'types' the command to one or more charges to fire, bursting the blood sachets and tearing the actor's clothing (which has previously been cut and loosely re-sewn).

'We call it "squibbing",' explains Chenakee. 'We use the same technique for war films when we want to simulate machine-gun bullets hitting a wall. We drill a line of holes, put in the charges, plug them with putty and then use the "typewriter" to set them off in sequence.'

Next, a secret of *McMillan and Wife*. 'Rock Hudson doesn't do the driving,' confesses Chenakee. 'He hires a double to do it for him. And because the double enjoys car stunts, there are lots of chases in the series.'

Hudson rarely goes to San Francisco. Nearly all the scenes are shot at Universal Studios and then cunningly faked to make them look as though the stars have been on location. It saves money.

One technique – 'matt processing' – involves an artist called Albert Whitlock and some special attachments to the film camera known as 'opaque cut-outs'. Whitlock goes to the location, perhaps the Rocky Mountains or some district of New York, and paints the scene very realistically in oils. He is paid about £1,000 a painting. The paintings are then taken to Universal Studios. Meanwhile, an opaque cut-out, a kind of specially shaped glass mask, has been placed across the lens of the camera as the actors are filmed in Hollywood. The cut-out permits only part of the film to be exposed (say the lower half of the scene) on the first occasion. Then a reverse of the cut-out mask is placed across the camera as it is turned over again, this time filming Whitlock's painting. Camera and painting are carefully lined up and, as the film is exposed for a second time, the effect is given of the action taking place against the background of the Rocky Mountains or New York.

Some other Hollywood secrets:

Trees in Hollywood are often rolls of wire mesh to which bark has been attached. They may have no tops – only the trunks usually need to be seen – and are mounted on small trolleys which can be moved around sets quickly.

Brick walls are usually made out of foam rubber and then painted.

Grass is real grass but sprayed a shiny green to make it look healthy all year round, especially in summer when the temperature often tops 32°C in Hollywood.

Fog is created by mixing petroleum distillate with distilled water, heated together inside a fog machine which ejects it as a cloud to drift about. Ground mist is usually made by spraying solid carbon dioxide blocks with hot mineral oil.

Snow is made by two different methods. A gentle fall of snowflakes come from a chicken wire drum, filled with shavings of white plastic and rotated overhead. Snowdrifts, or a carpet of snow, are made by whipping up soap suds and spraying them evenly on the ground.

The crunch of footsteps in the snow is created by men in the Special Effects section walking on cornflakes in time with the actor's footsteps.

Rain is created by garden sprinklers pointed upwards – allowing the water to fall naturally back to earth. The water is tinted – bright blue for daytime rain, or mixed with milk for night scenes – so that it looks real (ordinary, clear water tends to show up like scratches on film).

Model makers

Working in every special effects team are skilled model makers – men like Southern Television's Dennis Rowlands. The task he remembers best was fashioning an extraordinary set of crazy inventions for the comedy *Bright's Boffins*.

Most of the things for *Bright's Boffins* were meant to go wrong, like the ticker tape machine and the computer which poured beer and sixpences. For the computer Mr Rowlands used a real beer pump, a one-armed bandit and some video-tape reels.

Electrical engineer Bill Garrett is the genius behind the tiny models used on *Sooty* and *Sooty and Sweep* shows.

All the things Bill has made for Sooty are kept in a village school in Menston, near Ilkley, and part of the school is used as Sooty's rehearsal rooms.

There are literally thousands of props and television 'sets' in the school. Most of them have only been used once – and then for about five minutes.

They include a talking parrot in a pet shop, a barrel organ, a cobbler's shop and a vacuum cleaner which blows out flowers instead of cleaning. He takes greatest pride, however, in Sooty's deep-sea fishing trawler – complete with lifeboat and net.

The Graphics Department

Models also come within the scope of the Graphics Department in television. The ingenuity of most Graphics Artists is marvellous to watch. Matchsticks, cardboard, polystyrene, paper clips, glue, poster paints and stencils – these are the humble raw materials they rely on. Yet the visual results they obtain can transform a programme into a memorable event.

Whether written, printed, diagrammatic, pictorial or originally designed, graphics have a place in nearly every TV programme. For a start, most of the programme titles and 'end credits' – lists of people involved in the production – are designed by the Graphics Department. These are usually presented on a 'roller caption' machine.

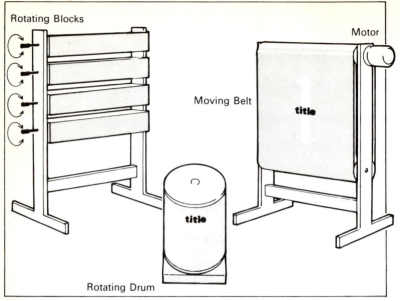

Caption machines

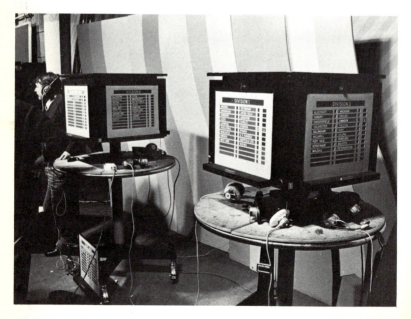

Football scores being mounted for **World of Sport**

The roller caption machine is rather like a mangle: it may be hand-turned or motor-driven. The roller – the drum on which the lettering is either laid flat or made to stand out – can be rotated horizontally or vertically. Or the lettering may be fixed to a set of parallel, rotating strips, or printed onto a sheet wound between two rollers. Each method produces a different effect on the TV screen.

Lettering comes in many different styles, each style carefully chosen to suit the programme. Factual, current affairs-type programmes call for formal lettering; drama or vaudeville shows are better suited by more ornate titles. Lettering may be used on its own, against a plain background, or super-imposed ('supered') over a picture or a drawing on a card.

The cards used by graphics artists vary in size but have a four (in length) to three (in height) ratio to fill the TV screen. The most common card size is 30 cm by 23 cm. For easy reading, lettering should be at least one twenty-fifth of the screen height which means, in practice, no smaller than three centimetres.

Letters may be hand-drawn, printed, transferred, electronically typed or photo-set. A revolution in TV graphics occurred some 15 years ago with the development of dry-transfers and the introduction of photo-setting, both of which reduced the time taken to produce many types of graphics to a fraction of its previous length. Another revolution may be about to occur with the introduction of the Aston character generator (which generates characters electronically) and a machine called Chiron.

Chiron is an electronic typewriter with a variety of type-faces and a facility to print in colour as well as black-and-white. It also has a 'memory' – a disc on which it is possible to set up words or symbols and store them until wanted on the TV screen. The operator sits at a keyboard and types out the information or lettering needed. This is then fed electronically either directly onto the TV screen or as a 'super' (super-imposed caption) in any of 24 different sorts of type, in any of six different sizes and any of six different colours. It can be fed immediately – as the operator touches the keys – or stored for as long as necessary and then released at the push of a button.

Literally thousands of pieces of information can be stored and indexed as captions: the operator simply dials up the appropriate number from the index. The information can then be flashed immediately onto the screen or placed on stand-by.

The first Chiron in Britain was installed at Independent Television News' studios in Wells Street, London in the summer of 1973. Possibly its most dramatic use so far was during the joint flights of the US Apollo and Russian Soyuz spaceships in 1975. Frank Miles of the ITN Space Unit was able to pre-set, in Chiron, the names of all the towns in Britain and Europe over which the two spaceships were passing

Graphic Artist at work

during the few minutes in which the historic handshake between the two crew commanders was taking place.

While the TV cameras showed the scene inside the cabins and microphones picked up the words of the astronauts 'live', ITV viewers were able to receive silent information about what was happening through the medium of Chiron.

Caption after caption – 'Now approaching Cornwall', 'Passing over Okehampton' and the now-famous 'Over Bognor now' – rippled across the base of the screen, interfering neither with picture nor sound.

This illustrates an important principle in TV graphics – they should never be redundant but used only to add something which the viewer is not getting from other sources. Used properly, they can create an extra dimension to the picture on the screen.

Chiron is an expensive machine. The one at ITN cost nearly £18,000. Its effectiveness is greatest in a situation where graphic information needs to be up-dated frequently and at speed – as, for instance, when election or sports results have to be displayed or silent explanations given to support rapidly-changing pictures on the screen. In such a role, it has no competitor. But this kind of display of information is but one of the many requirements placed before TV graphics artists: they may be asked for diagrams, charts, animated captions, fancy lettering or even models.

As far as lettering is concerned it is now common practice to use dry ink-transfer systems (such as Letraset or Transplus) in which a sheet of pre-inked letters or symbols is selected from stock and then transferred on to cardboard by burnishing the required character with a pencil or stick. Firms producing these transfers offer a range of sizes and type-faces. The resulting graphics, if arranged carefully, are uniformly neat.

Another method is to photo-set the letters or symbols. This involves sending the piece of artwork away to a specialist printer. The TV graphics artist chooses his style and type-size from a catalogue and indicates the lay-out required: the photo-setter makes a negative and then a black-and-white bromide print. Lettering may be deliberately distorted – compressed or elongated – if desired, using this technique. The advantage of the method is that the graphics artist does not have to position each letter or symbol manually – a machine does it for him, with greater precision.

A third (after Chiron possibly the fastest way of producing captions for the TV screen) is to use a 'hot press'. Brass letters are laid face down over a bed of metal on which a card, covered by a sheet of plastic foil, has been placed. A handle is pulled, clamping a hot plate onto the backs of the brass letters: the resultant heat is conducted through the metal to melt the plastic slightly, pressing ink on its underside onto the card below. Using this technique, it would be possible to produce an immaculate caption in two minutes flat compared with five minutes if Letraset or Transplus were used.

Other forms of lettering may be hand-drawn or sculpted out of a variety of materials. Shadows, reflections and silhouettes are sometimes used to give a slightly ethereal effect: three-dimensional words may be created out of more solid substances such as wood, plastic, strips of metal, string – even shaving cream. Sticks, stones, drawing pins or patches of cloth may be arranged to give novelty to a caption, also, or lines may be drawn in sand, icing sugar or foam.

Animated captions call for real imagination on the part of the artist: not only do they have to illustrate, graphically, the message but they must be constructed in such a way as to be easily operated by staff in the studio. If pieces of cardboard have to be pulled or revolved, fingers or strings must remain invisible. Sometimes, parts of the caption are made of metal so that they can be moved invisibly by magnets from the rear.

The Casting Director

For many types of TV production it is the researcher's job to select suitable people to appear on the programme: but with drama and light entertainment the task is usually given to the Casting Director.

The Casting Director has not only to fit the right actor or actress to the right part but also to keep finding a regular supply of new talent.

The Casting Director's 'bible' is the *Spotlight Casting Directory* which lists the names, descriptions, agents and addresses of more than 8,000 actors and actresses. But he has many other reference sources, apart from his own contacts book and memory. Several agencies exist to supply particular types of performers for specialist roles – people whose names and faces will rarely become known to viewers because they are only required occasionally for 'bit' parts.

One such agency – perhaps the most bizarre of all – glories in the name of Ugly Enterprises Ltd. It supplies ugly people, or people of unusual dimensions, such as dwarfs or huge men. On its books are the tallest man in Britain (Christopher Greener, 2 metres 30 centimetres, the second-fattest man in Britain (John Robinson, 227 kilos), a woman with 152-centimetre hips, hunchbacks, people with tumours and 'port wine stains' on their faces, men with elongated noses or missing eyes.

Once the Casting Director has found his performer, he negotiates a fee – generally giving more money to a person whose name is likely to induce the viewer to watch than to an unknown. Frequently, the negotiation is done through an agent.

The agent is a vital link between artist and programme company – a protective buffer who often has to work hard for his 10 per cent. Agents handling top performers usually have a script sent to them for approval before any agreement is made: then, if it appeals, negotiations begin over fees, 'billings' and 'credits'. 'Billings' are publicity given in advance of a programme. 'Credits' are titles on the screen.

Some agents act as personal managers as well, handling all the artists' problems, personal as well as professional. In return, they may take as much as 50 per cent of the fee. Others specialise in representing 'bit-part' actors and actresses – otherwise known as 'walk-ons' or 'noddies' (because they speak no lines but are allowed to nod).

A 'noddy' is paid £15 a day. If he speaks three words, the fee shoots up to £21 (1975 rates). Becoming a 'noddy' is often the best way for a young actor to break into television – the craft can be learned on the studio floor and, if all goes well, the performer can graduate to larger parts and (with his agent's help) to bigger fees.

If the Casting Director has done his job properly, he will rarely appear on 'the set' – except possibly to watch some newcomer at work.

The Make-up Department

Everywhere that TV artists go, the Make-up Department follows. The basic make-up used includes dry 'cakes' of compressed powder, a creamy but non-greasy base (usually taken from jars or small stick-containers), a grease-paint foundation (in tubes) and powder or liquid bases.

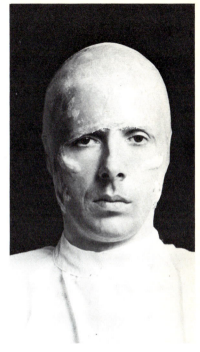

The science of make-up ... actor Richard O'Sullivan (top left, in real life) acts as subject for a complicated make-up job – a living skull, created by Thames TV make-up experts as part of a demonstration of television techniques, given at the Victoria and Albert Museum in 1975

The make-up artist's tools include small sponges, chamois leathers, wax pencils and brushes – sometimes even a palette knife, for when 'surface modelling' is called for.

'Surface modelling' means changing the physical contours of the flesh. Plastic substances may be squeezed out of a tube to produce scars or ridges. Or a mixture of pyroxylin, alcohol and ether – known as 'inflexible collodion' – may be brushed on, layer by layer, to contract the flesh and make it rise locally.

'Fish skin' may also be used to alter contours to a minor degree. Resembling the skin of a fish in texture, it is actually a transparent plastic (rather like Cellotape) which can be fixed into place using spirit gum. It is often used to give an impression of Oriental eyes or to cover folds of flesh.

For major transformations of the face, masks, morticians' wax, plasticine or nose-putty are used, sometimes with pads of cotton wool, tissue paper or sponge. Often the area to be padded is brushed first with '*flexible* collodion' – a mixture of resin, castor oil, alcohol and ether – which tends to make the skin stretch or expand so that the attachment grips better and is comfortable. Warts, eye-bags, wounds or extra-large noses are often produced in this way.

Where a performer's own hair is unsuitable, hair pieces or toupées can be attached to the scalp: in the case of women, 'postiche' (pinned-on) hair can provide extra ringlets, buns or tresses. Sometimes, if hair is rather dark and lifeless, extra life is given to it by powdering it with gold or silver dust.

The variety and combination of make-up used depends on three things: the performer's own features and colouring, the character to be portrayed and the lighting. Natural daylight, for example, calls for different make-up from studio lighting. A sinister character demands different make-up from a fresh-faced, open or honest personality.

Make-up girls are usually looked on as ministering angels by TV performers, not simply because they have the skill to 'make a silk purse out of a sow's ear' but because their soothing touch and friendly re-assurance comes at a time when most performers are beginning to feel some degree of tension.

Wardrobe

But just as important, in the army of backroom personalities, are the Wardrobe Staff: seamstresses, dressers, supervisors. They are responsible for costumes and clothing. They may make up outfits themselves, take them 'off the peg' or hire them. Tape measure, needles and cotton are the tools of their trade.

The Wardrobe Department's staff have to know how to dye materials, wash and iron, as well as stitch the garments themselves. The Wardrobe Supervisor works with the Director anything up to two

months before a show, planning the style and colours of the clothes
before measuring up and fitting the artists. A range of standard garments – modern suits, dresses, night clothes, skirts, jackets and blouses
– is usually hired from specialist costumiers. The largest suppliers of
costumes for TV, films and the theatre – Bermans and Nathans Ltd –
boast more than 10,000 garments in stock in a warehouse covering
25,000 square metres.

Stunt artists

Fights with weapons or with animals are rarely done by actors themselves. Electronic techniques – such as 'split screen' effects or
Chromakey – make it possible, sometimes, for an illusion to be given
of an animal in action, especially if it is supposed to attack a human.
On other occasions, a stunt man may be used in place of the actor.

There are more than 200 stunt artists registered with Equity, the
actors' union, and more than a dozen stunt directors. The stunt directors work out the actions needed in a stunt: the stunt artists perform it
– usually as a part-time occupation. It may be a sword fight or falling
down stairs, jumping off a building, being 'killed' in a gun fight,
mauled by a panther, crashing a car, or just plain standing at the
receiving end of a powerful 'sock' on the jaw. Most are men, although
about 20 are women and, in America, there is a Stuntwoman's
Association as well.

Animals on the screen

Finding animals to appear on television calls for another kind of skill.
Mary Chipperfield runs one such service.

With her father, former circus boss Jimmy Chipperfield, her 'family'
of animal actors includes 300 lions (Mary's husband, Roger Cawley,
manages the Marquess of Bath's Lions of Longleat), 12 tigers, two
leopards, six llamas, 75 elephants, a black panther, two ostriches, six
white rhinos, a giraffe, four Great Danes, two Alsatians, a score of
cats, five chimpanzees, three pythons and a Giant Condor. She trains
most of them herself.

Once, she took a tiger to Thames Television's studios at
Teddington. It was supposed to be seen in a dungeon awaiting a
victim as part of an episode in a Sherlock Holmes TV series. Mary and
her husband got into position behind some scenery, holding the tiger
on a chain.

Suddenly a studio technician used a clapperboard to signal the start
of filming. Mary recalls vividly what happened next: 'In a flash, the
tiger was off – dragging us across the studio and knocking down a
whole lot of scenery and lights. You've never seen a film crew vanish
so quickly!'

TV companies can hire a lion for £150 a day, an elephant for £200, a horse for between £25 and £150, a dog for £20 – or even a mouse for £20. Why is a mouse so expensive? 'Because all our animals have to be accompanied by at least two handlers (lions get four) and the fee includes transport costs as well as insurance.'

Because top TV stars are often involved in scenes with the animals, Mary is obliged to carry 'third party' insurance of up to £500,000. Training an animal may take six months.

Many different tricks are used to get the animals to act in the way the plot demands. 'To get snakes to move where you want them, for example, the best thing is to surround them with bright lights but to leave a corner in darkness,' she explains. 'The snake will usually crawl towards the darkness.'

Mice are directed by making noise behind them, 'luring them with cheese takes far too long.' Elephants are coaxed with sugar, cattle nuts or sticky buns. Lions are shown first where to go – then attracted to the spot with meat on the end of a stick.

'The most difficult animal to train for TV or films,' says Mary, 'is the domestic cat. It's so unintelligent. Furthermore, cats don't like working under lights. You have to keep rewarding them with tit-bits and then, on the day before they are due to go in front of the cameras, cut their rations, so that they are really hungry when recording starts.'

Graphic designers, scenery builders, 'props' and special effects men, make-up artists, wardrobe keepers, stunt actors, location specialists, animal trainers, programme researchers, scriptwriters – add to these the actual production team and the host of secretaries, receptionists, accounts clerks, security guards, canteen staff, car drivers, maintenance engineers, casting specialists, personnel and publicity officers, programme executives and Board Members – and it may help to explain why it now costs an average of £200 per minute of television seen on the screen.

Chapter 5
'On air'

It is now possible for 99 out of every 100 people in Britain to receive television. By 1976, more than 40 per cent of the population had actually bought a TV set and something like 85 per cent were known to be watching regularly. From the total of 29 TV sets sold in 1929, the figure had reached 20 million by the time this book was written, 52 per cent of them colour sets.

The number of broadcasting hours had increased, too, from 20 hours a week in 1936 to more than 90.

In less than 50 years, therefore, television has transformed itself from a curiosity into a national institution – an accepted part of daily life. And the credit, to a very large extent, is due to the engineers and technicians who set the standards for transmission and maintain the transmitters.

The most entertaining or interesting programme is not worth watching if reception is poor: television engineers work literally night and day to ensure that reception is good. All over Britain, tall, slender towers and masts rise gracefully above mountains, ridges, escarpments and moors, beaming the unseen picture and sound signals across the country, lifting them out of harm's way and ensuring that they meet no worse interference than the air we breathe: millions of signals every minute, all perfectly synchronised to produce clear, faithful pictures on 20 million screens.

Be it a documentary, a play, or a spectacular, to bring the action from the studio to your television set at home involves routeing the signal along a complex path of control centres, switching centres, links and transmitters, as well as making careful checks at points along the route to ensure that a high quality signal is maintained. The whole process involves many operations and personnel, as well as millions of pounds worth of electronic equipment.

The studio camera provides the first link in this 'on air' chain. If the programme is recorded, video tape recorders or telecine machines replace the camera, at the time of transmission, as the originator of the signal. There may be additional caption scanners and many different microphones for sound in use, also, in one programme.

As I have indicated, the programme Director and his assistants compose and assemble the whole programme by selecting from these sources and the signal then passes to Master Control. In Master Control, or its equivalent, announcements or advertisements are inserted at the correct times, network 'hook-ups' completed and the signal checked for quality.

It is at this point that the Post Office takes over. It rents links between the production centres and the transmitters. To the IBA alone, it rents some 7,240 kilometres of links which carry the colour signals from the studios to the giant aerials through a complex network of switching centres, microwave beams and cables. A typical ITV networked programme travels over several thousand kilometres of Post Office cable and through 15 Post Office switching centres before it even reaches the IBA's transmitters.

The Post Office Tower in London is one of the five main switching centres (the others are at Birmingham, Manchester, Carlisle, and Kirk o'Shotts near Glasgow) and over 700 switches a week are performed there, routeing different programmes to different BBC or ITV centres. The operation of the London switching centre is such that material from 30 different sources can be switched to any one of 80 different destinations. At the five main stations, switches are performed automatically to a pre-set timetable controlled by TIM, the Post Office clock.

The switching in the Post Office Tower – which also acts as an aerial mast for relaying signals – is performed inside a room known as the London-Television Network Switching Centre. Like Master Control, it is filled with monitor screens and banks of 'patch panels'. It is through here, also, that all TV programmes from overseas pass on their way to the British public – relayed from Eurovision or from satellites in space – and all British programmes on their way overseas.

TV pictures of the wedding of Captain Mark Phillips to Princess Anne passed through the Post Office Tower and went out to an audience estimated at hundreds of millions of people; TV pictures from the last Moon walk, the Israeli-Egyptian War, the Eurovision Song Contest came in.

The television network distribution equipment is completely automatic and, since the introduction of transistors, breaks are measured merely in seconds. In 1975, for example, the reliability of the service was 99·998 per cent.

The vast array of engineering systems inside the Tower are fascinating; but it is the Tower itself which captures the limelight. When it was designed, engineers decreed that it must not deviate from the upright by more than a third of a degree in any wind condition – otherwise the highly-directional aerials incorporated in it would be affected: half a degree, for instance, would be sufficient to cause a loss of reception, at the other end, of half the signal power. Wind tunnel tests and mathematical calculations made by scientists at the National Physical Laboratory predicted that this particular design would move 38 centimetres from the vertical, at the top, in winds of 175 kilometres per hour – within the 'third of a degree' limit. In practice, the maximum movement so far recorded has been 23 centimetres – in a gale of 145 kilometres per hour.

The transmitters

From switching centres like the Post Office Tower, the TV signal travels to the actual BBC and IBA transmitters for radiation to the public.

A television transmission is rather like the ripples on a pond after a stone has been thrown in. The energy is radiated outwards from the transmitter in the form of waves. The distance between the crests of the waves is known as the 'wavelength' and the number of waves passing any particular point in a second is known as the 'frequency'.

Frequencies are usually measured in 'cycles per second' or 'Hertz'.

Energy radiates from many things, in Nature. Each form of radiation has a different frequency. A DC (direct current) battery, for instance, has a frequency of zero. A star giving off gamma rays radiates that particular form of energy at a frequency of 10,000,000,000,000,000,000 cycles per second or Hertz.

Somewhere near the middle of this so-called 'energy spectrum' lie the frequencies used for broadcasting television – stretching from 41 million cycles per second (41 Mc/s) or Hertz (41 MHz) to 1,000 million cycles per second (1,000 Mc/s) or Hertz (1,000 MHz, otherwise known as one GigaHertz (1 GHz)).

Engineers classify these frequencies by splitting them into three – Very High Frequencies (VHF), Ultra-High Frequencies (UHF) and Super-High Frequencies (SHF). VHF is used nowadays for the transmission of 405-line television, UHF for 625-line, and SHF for short-distance links between outside broadcast units and the studio.

The three broad categories have been subdivided into five 'Bands' – Bands I, II, III, IV and V.

Band I, which ranges from 41 to 68 Mega Hertz (41–68 MHz), is used exclusively by the BBC for transmission of 405-line, black and white programmes; Band III, which stretches from 174 to 216 MHz on the frequency scale, is mostly used by ITV for its 405-line transmissions; Band IV (470–582 MHz) and Band V (614–854 MHz) are available jointly to both networks for 625-line colour programmes. Band II is reserved for sound broadcasting by both the IBA and the BBC.

Each of these Bands is further subdivided into 'Channels', which are even narrower bands of frequencies. Each is given a number. The BBC's Crystal Palace transmitter, for example, broadcasts 405-line television on Channel 1 of Band I; the IBA's 405-line transmitter at Croydon operates on Channel 9 of Band III. The higher Bands on the Ultra High Frequencies (UHF) contain more Channels – Band IV, for example, can accommodate 14 Channels whilst Band V can accommodate 30 – the only proviso being that each Channel, or television programme, must be separated by a minimum of 8 MHz of frequency spacing to prevent overlap and, therefore, interference between programmes.

Because regional TV programmes are often different, quite a lot of juggling has to be done with Channels, around the country, so that transmitters do not interfere with one another to an unacceptable degree.

In Yorkshire, for example, the IBA's transmitters at Cop Hill, Hebden Bridge, Oxenhope and Wharfedale all beam out on Channel 25, while those at Calver Peak and Skipton use Channel 49 and those at Heyshaw and Tideswell Moor occupy Channel 60. Such selections dovetail in with BBC Channels so that the two networks do not interfere with each other.

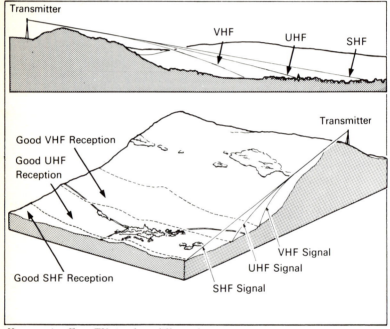

How terrain affects TV signals at different frequencies

Each set of frequencies has its own characteristics: those which cause engineers concern are the degree to which signal strength falls off with distance from the transmitter and the extent to which the signals will 'bend' around or over obstructions. On VHF, for example, the waves will, to some extent, swirl around solid obstructions and bend over the horizon. On UHF, the effect is far less pronounced: there is virtually no bending and solid obstructions tend to produce 'shadows' – areas where reception is impossible or poor. Considerable extra transmitting power is called for to help overcome this – often eight to ten times more power than for VHF – and considerably more transmitters.

In fact, the hilly nature of much of Britain's countryside has meant that the number of transmitters needed to give national coverage on UHF is some four or five times as great as for VHF. On SHF, this screening problem becomes even more pronounced. Coverage can virtually only be given if the aerials are within sight of each other.

All this may help to explain why, with 95 per cent of the population receiving its television from 150 or so transmitting stations, it may require a further 250 if the remaining five per cent are to be fully covered. They may never be, of course. As Howard Steele, Director of Engineering of the Independent Broadcasting Authority, which builds, owns and operates all the ITV transmitters, put it to me, 'There comes a point at which it becomes prohibitively expensive to serve small pockets of people, or individuals, with TV. Even a small transmitter today costs at least £40,000. Our present policy is to build one only if it can serve at least 400 homes. Even so, that works out at £100 a home compared with, say, the original figure of nine pence a home in the London area, where a single transmitter can serve nearly 11 million people.'

The IBA's 405-line (black-and-white) VHF service covers 98·7 per cent of the population, via 21 high-powered transmitters and 26 relay stations of lower power, built to fill in the gaps. The BBC's VHF service covers a slightly larger proportion – 99·5 per cent – using 27 high-powered transmitters and 84 relays. Of these, 64 transmitters have had to be built to reach less than one per cent of the total potential audience.

For beaming UHF (625-line, colour) TV programmes, sites and aerial masts are being shared by both networks and building divided on a 50–50 basis. By the time the UHF network is completed, some 52 main stations and 450 relays will have been constructed at a rate of more than one a week. By 1980, Britain should be the best-served nation in Europe as far as TV is concerned.

It is costing the IBA and BBC about £3–4 millions a year each to install new transmitters – in the case of the IBA, about one quarter of its total expenditure.

Many of the transmitters, including all those built for relaying UHF transmissions by the IBA, are unmanned. The smaller ones contain solid-state equipment which needs little maintenance and which can be housed in one room – a standard, square hut, pre-fabricated out of steel and placed on a concrete slab below the aerial. Transmitters are duplicated, so that if one breaks down, the programme switches automatically to the other.

The use of these special container buildings – known to engineers as '10–S Containers' – means that much of the work of constructing a transmitter can be done in workshops away from the installation point, which may be remote, weather-beaten country.

A new transmitter of the '10–S Container' type arrives on the back of a lorry and is lowered into position under the aerial mast. Some 500 of these are being installed in Britain each year

One of the IBA's flying squads of engineers who service and repair TV transmitters. The estate car carries £20,000 wort of equipment

The first of these solid-state container stations – putting out only 10 watts but relaying TV signals three or four kilometres in all directions – was installed at Morpeth in 1974. Some 500 are now going into position each year.

To service the unattended transmitters, the IBA Engineering Division, whose headquarters are at Crawley Court near Winchester, set up its own 'flying squad' of engineers. Each two-man team has an estate car containing some £20,000 worth of special test equipment, and is geared to rush quickly across many kilometres to rectify a fault. The working lives of these engineers are spent often in remote places on hill tops or in buildings under the shadows of masts towering 300 metres or more into the sky.

Main transmitters are more complex. Nobody has yet developed transistorised equipment good enough to boost TV signals of even 1,000, much less 80,000 watts (in the case of the Crystal Palace transmitter), and so giant valves called klystrons still have to be used. These require elaborate cooling systems. The heat is made to turn water into steam, which is then allowed to evaporate.

The Crystal Palace aerials have to radiate up to a million watts of power. A special design of building was called for, partly embedded underground. Two Marconi 40 kilowatt transmitters were installed, each with its own cooling and silencing system. Yet the whole station is left to run by itself, unattended except for an occasional inspection.

The very first ITV programmes went out from transmitters generating a mere 10,000 watts. They were beamed from West Norwood, near Croydon. Some idea of what conditions were like in those days may be gleaned from Phil Darby who became the station's first Senior Shift Engineer.

'I reported for duty at the Croydon site in early September 1955,' Mr Darby recalls, 'to find a scene of splendid disorder. The single pair of prototype transmitters was being installed. The prefabricated building offered few creature comforts but it was at least weatherproof. Five of the staff had previously seen a television transmitter but no-one had any experience of Band III broadcast equipment.

'My confidence was not enhanced when I learned that the second pair of transmitters would not be available for many months and that no handbooks and only a few "back-of-the envelope" circuit diagrams were available to explain the mysteries of the prototype equipment. At this stage, we were obliged to prepare our own circuit diagrams of the more important units. After a few days, we were able to commence power tests. The vision transmitter was a miscellaneous collection of odd components. To apply power to the final amplifier was a feat requiring skill, courage and perhaps some acrobatic ability. One had to close the switch with the right hand whilst disabling the overload trip device with the left foot.

'Not only technical problems had to be solved. The lawns needed grooming and we built the original "rotary" mower using ground-down hacksaw blades to provide the business end of the machine.'

Mr Darby adds, 'In spite of the somewhat insecure transmitter situation the early programmes and commercials were of splendid quality both technically and otherwise. Only one really serious break-down occurred during the early period. This took place on a Sunday evening, when the sound transmitter tripped just before the *Palladium Show* was due to start. Since there was no other transmitter, the show had to be delayed for an hour and a half until the fault was located and repaired. For the whole of this period Tommy Trinder ad-libbed to the invited theatre audience. He then compered the show as if nothing had happened. The following week he appeared on stage with a large bag of workman's tools and offered to fix it himself should another breakdown occur. (I always knew those programme chaps thought that engineers were "over-paid" plumbers.)

'Apart from these incidents, the equipment worked well and stayed on the air with remarkable consistency, provided that we washed the Combining Unit air filters every 20 minutes or so to remove the London grime!'

Television aerial masts come in a variety of shapes and sizes; some are all-metal, others partly concrete. It is the function of the transmitting aerial to radiate a combined signal – the electro-magnetic carrier wave and the sound-and-vision signals coming from the studio – in the desired direction or directions. Some are more directional than others, depending on the terrain and community they have to serve.

Masts range in height from 50 to 420 metres. Some aerial arrays fixed to the masts may themselves be 30 metres tall and each part of the aerial is very carefully designed and constructed. Broadly speaking, there are three parts to every aerial – the radiating elements, the main feeder cables which carry the radio-frequency power from the transmitters to the top of the mast, and distribution feeders which divide the power and feed it to the individual aerial elements. As much as half the transmitter's output may be lost in getting the power up the aerial mast.

The largest TV aerial in Britain belongs to the IBA and stands on Emley Moor in Yorkshire. This slender and graceful giant, weighing more than 16,000 tonnes, carries the IBA's UHF and VHF aerials which bring Yorkshire Television to the homes of nearly six million people. It is the third largest in Europe after those in East Berlin and Moscow. It is more than twice the height of London's Post Office Tower.

The pattern of radiation given off by a transmitting aerial is called a 'polar diagram' and it is rather like the contour lines on an Ordnance Survey map. The contour indicates the signal strength and the cover-

A UHF transmitter aerial (inset)
The largest TV aerial in Britain – the IBA transmitter on Emley Moor, Yorkshire

age given on the ground and different lay-outs of aerial elements will produce different polar diagrams.

Home aerials

The electro-magnetic radiation leaving the aerial goes out in waves. Depending on the direction in which the elements of the aerial are inclined – they may be pointed upright or laid horizontally – these waves are said to be either 'vertically polarized' or 'horizontally polarized'. It is extremely important that the rods or elements of the

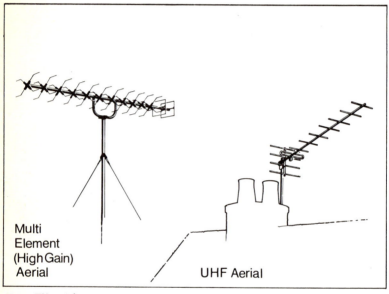

Multi
Element
(High Gain)
Aerial   UHF Aerial

Home TV aerials

viewer's aerial at home are placed in the same plane in order to ensure good reception. This means that, in some areas, the rods should be mounted vertically and in others horizontally. Broadly speaking, main transmitters use horizontal polarization (therefore viewers served by a main transmitter will need horizontal aerials) whilst relay stations use vertical (and therefore should be received by aerials pointing upwards). If a relay station opens in an area previously served by a main station, the aerial will need adjusting or changing. (The actual number of elements in the viewer's aerial will depend on such things as distance from the transmitter, power and radiation characteristics of the transmitter, and the nature of the intervening ground.)

To help viewers, the IBA issues guidance for the installation of home aerials. Advice can also be obtained from a local television dealer. As the IBA puts it:

'It is false economy to make do with an aerial unsuitable for your location. Although the very simple "set-top" aerial may sometimes provide sufficient signals in districts close to a transmitter, such reception will often be marred by the effect of people moving in the room, or cars passing the house.

'These effects can usually be avoided by using a loft or, better still, a high outside aerial. On VHF, a set-top aerial may sometimes be satisfactory within a few kilometres of a high-power transmitter. But for UHF – and especially for colour reception – a good outdoor or loft aerial should always be fitted.'

The simplest practical form of receiving aerial comprises a single dipole element, but additional signal gain and directivity (that is, the ability of an aerial to reject signals from other than the desired direction) is achieved by adding extra elements – 'directors' and 'reflectors' – so as to form an aerial array.

A typical VHF array might comprise four red elements (dipole plus reflector and two directors) and this would be known as a four-element aerial.

The more elements an aerial comprises, the more it will normally cost and the stronger will need to be the supports. This means that an aerial will usually be chosen in accordance with the signal available in the particular district. For aerial elements it is truly a matter of 'not too few – not too many – but just right'.

Whether a viewer gets good or bad reception depends, in the main, on two things: his distance from the transmitter and the size and position of intervening obstacles, such as hills and tall buildings. Main transmitters usually radiate for 48–65 kilometres or more: relay stations may only cover a radius of 3 to 5 kilometres. Nevertheless, local phenomena may still have an effect.

A hill or building may cause 'ghosting'. A 'ghost' image is brought about by signals reaching the receiving aerial after reflection off the obstacle, having travelled along a slightly different path from those coming directly from the transmitter. The main image is spoiled by a secondary, 'ghost' image – just to its right – on the screen. Such 'ghosting' can usually be removed or greatly reduced by improving the directivity of the home aerial.

Another form of distortion is 'co-channel interference'. This usually only bothers viewers at certain times of the year, during a weather condition known as 'inversion', but it results in receivers picking up signals from distant transmitters working on the same channel – sometimes from abroad. Patterns on the screen in the form of diagonal stripes of light and dark shade, or sound interference, may result. The phenomenon usually is limited to areas where the local signal is weak and usually only lasts for a few hours.

Weakness of the signal is usually the diagnosis if the picture on the home screen is 'grainy' or 'noisy'. Improvement or adjustment of the aerial can often remedy it.

A 'snowstorm' on the screen may mean that the picture signal is being affected by local electrical interference.

Any apparatus, motor vehicle, switches, plugs or sockets which produce electrical sparks, no matter how minute, can be the cause of interference unless this spark is damped out by means of correctly designed and installed interference suppression filters on the offending apparatus.

Good reception

'Ghosting'

Weak signal

Co-channel interference

Local interference

Some common picture faults

In the UK, Parliament has introduced legislation which restricts the amount of interference which can be legally produced by new equipment; however, equipment which may have been satisfactory when first installed can sometimes deteriorate and become the source of interference. Electrical interference to television usually takes the form of a severe 'snowstorm' of light or dark tiny random spots on all or part of the screen.

When the source of interference appears to be somewhere outside the home, and it is reasonably certain that it is electrical interference and not a fault in the receiver, it may be advisable to ask the Post Office to help. This can be done by filling in a T113G form, *Good Radio and Television Reception*, obtainable from any main Post Office.

Post Office investigation officers will then usually call; they have the experience and apparatus necessary to help them detect the source of the interference, or to advise on any steps to be taken.

Finally, a wavy pattern of lines on the screen, when the set is tuned to UHF, may be caused by a nearby TV receiver being tuned to a VHF station.

On the whole, the quality of the TV picture received in Britain is exceptionally good compared with the rest of the world. This is, to a large measure, due to the setting of extremely high standards for the design and performance of equipment by both the BBC and the IBA and to the painstaking monitoring of signals by engineers along the route from studio to home. There are separate transmitters for vision and sound: each is painstakingly checked for quality. There is a chain of monitoring points – in the Control Room, in Master Control, in the Regional Control Centres, in the Post Office switching centres and finally in the headquarters of the Engineering Divisions of both authorities – each casting a critical eye over what is happening.

The TV signal – from studio to home

Let us finally trace, then, what happens to the TV signal from creation to reception.

The separate sound and video signals leave the studio and pass through the first engineering control. But before they do, a vital addition is made – the 'Sync Pulse'.

The Sync Pulse – or synchronising signal – is a timing device which tells each camera tube or picture scanner where to end one 'line' of the TV picture and begin the next; it also makes sure that all the equipment is in unison.

The Master Sync Pulse Generator, as it is known, contains a very stable and accurate oscillator which generates a pulse 20,250 times a second for a 405-line picture or 31,250 times a second for 625-lines. These pulses are fed through various other electronic components with titles such as 'frequency divider' and 'field blanking pulse generator' which marshall them so that a total of precisely 25 separate pictures is completed on the TV screen every second. The generator and its ancillary equipment are usually housed in the Central Apparatus Room, some way away from the actual studio.

Engineers monitor the precisely-assembled signal as it comes into and leaves the Studio Control Room, and as it enters and leaves Master Control. It then goes by cable or microwave relay to the transmitter. On the way, it is monitored by Post Office engineers. At the transmitter, it is put onto the back of a carrier wave.

The carrier wave is generated by an oscillator, stepped up in a frequency multiplier, boosted by an RF amplifier and then fed to a modulator, where the video signal from the studio has also been amplified several times. At each stage in the chain, quality is checked against standards laid down by the BBC or IBA Engineering Divisions – standards of brightness and colour, resolution and registration.

The 'vision signal', as the combined carrier wave and studio picture signal is now called, is then joined by the sound signal. This is done in a 'combining unit' and the two signals are then fed to the aerial for transmission to the viewer.

Still the checks are not ended. Every single transmission is carefully logged and assessed for quality by engineers at the IBA regional headquarters. Separate assessments are given for vision and sound and a six-point quality scale is used: 1. Excellent, 2. Good, 3. Fairly good, 4. Rather poor, 5. Poor, 6. Very poor. Any faults have to be notified to the company responsible for them, and then investigated or explained.

Once again, the report forms carry a special jargon – 'beam flutter', 'black crushing', 'breathing', 'drop outs', 'gate static', 'grey scale mistracking', 'line jitter', to name but a few of the phrases used to describe picture faults and 'booming', 'buzz', 'flutter' and 'plops' to mention just some of those used for sound.

Chapter 6
Audience research and advertising

A constant contact is maintained with the public through the medium of the Audience Research Departments. Although the prime concern of the researcher is to find out how viewers *enjoy* particular programmes, a certain amount of comment about technical quality also filters back.

The BBC goes about its audience research rather differently from ITV. It conducts a continuous *Survey of Listening and Viewing* but it only questions individuals. ITV researchers deal with *households*. This explains why the two sets of audience figures sometimes differ.

Each day's BBC 'sample' consists of 2,250 people, selected to be representative of the whole population but excluding children under five. The questions put by interviewers – most of whom are women working part-time – all refer to the previous day and are designed to find out whether or not the interviewee listened to the radio or TV and, if so, to which particular programmes.

Different people are interviewed each day. In a month, about 70,000 are interviewed. The end-product, the *Daily Audience Barometer*, is the BBC's equivalent of the box office. It lists every programme broadcast and shows the proportions of the sample which viewed them.

The *opinions* of audiences are gathered through panels of listeners and viewers. Altogether their membership totals about 6,000. Panel members are recruited through public invitation and by personal approach.

Each week the panel member receives questionnaires about forthcoming broadcasts. He is not asked to vary his normal listening or viewing habits – indeed he is particularly requested not to do so, for the object is always to find out what people think of the programmes they choose in the ordinary way. The questionnaires, which vary in form, seek frank expressions of opinion, the briefest simply asking the panel member to rate the programme in different ways, for example, to indicate for a comedy programme to what extent it was funny or unfunny, vulgar or clean, and so on, and to sum up their reactions using another simple scale. This leads to Reaction Indices by means of which programmes can be readily compared with one another. Longer questionnaires provide material for the production of programme reports which try to give a balanced picture of the opinions expressed, placing correct emphasis both on the majority view and on the opinions of minorities.

ITV goes about it in a rather different way. It selects panels by random sample and measures their viewing habits on a minute-by-minute basis 2,650 houscholds and 7,790 individuals. Each household gets a 'SETmeter' which is attached to the TV set and individual 'Viewing Diaries' for each member of the household and any guests. The monitoring is carried out by Audits of Great Britain Ltd from its research centre, Audit House, at Eastcote, Middlesex.

The whole process of audience measurement starts on Monday morning when the housewife recovers the tape from the SETmeter and, together with the individual viewing diaries, posts it to AGB. Ninety per cent arrive safely by Tuesday morning, when the work of sorting the tapes and viewing diaries begins and the information is booked in by a cardex system. The next stage in the operation is to translate the information on the tape onto special punched paper tape capable of being read by the computer, a Honeywell 1200. This is done on an 'encoder'.

The viewing diaries, completed on a quarter-hour basis by each member of the household panel and any guests, are similarly transferred onto punched paper tape by means of a 'Lector'. Information from the programme logs of each of the ITV companies is then coded and put onto punched cards.

By Wednesday night, all of the information is available in a form suitable for the computer to digest and the process of feeding the Honeywell commences.

Thursday morning sees the computer drawing graphs, by means of an attachment called 'Calcomp', of the minute-by-minute audience levels for ITV and BBC for each day and for each ITV region. The computer also produces columns of viewing and cost information and these are pasted-up, checked and photographed before being printed on one of the eight machines at Audit House.

The last stage in the process is the collating and packing of individual reports prior to despatching them, on the Friday evening, to subscribers to the service, many of whom are advertisers or potential advertisers. Analyses are also made, breaking down the total audience for each channel into components which may be of special interest to advertisers, such as the social grouping of the audience.

A *Top Twenty* of programmes is drawn up each week. Such figures are an indication to advertisers of where they are likely to obtain best value for money and to programme planners of public taste. The price of advertising on ITV varies according to the likely size of audience. Thus, in 1975, it was possible to obtain a single 30-second commercial 'spot' for £1,500 in the early evening, for £7,500 at 7.30pm, for £10,000 just before *News at Ten*, or for £4,000 at 11.30pm.

The control over advertising

The actual nature and total of advertising on ITV is controlled by the IBA. The Independent Broadcasting Authority Act does not lay down precisely the amount of advertising that may be allowed: it simply places upon the IBA the duty to secure 'that the amount of time given to advertising in the programmes shall not be so great as to detract from the value of the programmes as a medium of information, education and entertainment'. Since the beginning of television transmissions in 1955, the Authority has allowed a maximum of six minutes of spot advertising an hour, averaged over the day's programmes. A further rule restricts the maximum, normally, to seven minutes in any single 'clock-hour' (e.g. from 6 to 7 pm, 7 to 8 pm). In radio, the maximum is nine minutes in any one clock-hour.

Some ITV programmes – indeed an average of 100 out of 180 in a typical week's viewing – carry no advertising at all: these include *This Week*, *World in Action*, schools programmes, religious programmes, some half-hour plays, some children's programmes and any programme lasting less than 20 minutes. Sixty programmes carry one commercial break. The remaining 20 carry two.

The commercial breaks are, of course, vital to the prosperity of ITV which has to pay for itself – none of the TV licence fee paid by the viewer is passed on to ITV companies which are also required to pay a Government Levy (up to 1975, this alone had totalled £217 millions). When commercial television first started in Britain 20 years ago, critics forecast that the public would become irritated by the breaks, even though, under the Act, they are supposed to be 'natural'. In reality the reverse has proved true. The majority of viewers not only appreciate opportunities to break away but enjoy the information and entertainment value of the ads.

There are over 20,000 new television advertisements a year. Of that number, 15,000 are from small local advertisers, mostly in the form of five- or seven-second slides, with very simple messages in vision and sound. Averaging a little over 1,000 a year in individual television areas, they publicize local stores, restaurants, transport services and other local enterprises and include announcements of vacancies by firms seeking staff, advertisements for local entertainment, sporting events, shows and fêtes. For this kind of publicity the local advertisers take up about six per cent of the available advertising time on average over the network. The rest of the new television advertisements each year are for a vast range of branded consumer goods and services. They come from thousands of advertisers – some directly, but for the most part through one or other of a great many advertising agencies – all with their own ideas of how their products can be presented in the best light and the most persuasive terms on the television screen.

The advertisers and agencies subscribe to voluntary codes of practice designed to raise standards of advertising through self-discipline in all media. It is recognised, however, that the use of such a powerful medium as television presents special problems and calls for a great degree of responsibility.

For this reason, the IBA has its own Advisory Committee on Advertising, its own Medical Advisory Panel and its own Advertising Control Division. It also has drawn up its own Code of Advertising Standards and Practice.

Amongst other things, this Code prohibits the showing of advertisements on TV for moneylenders, matrimonial agencies, undertakers, betting tipsters, bookmakers, private detective agencies, cigarettes and tobacco. It also excludes from advertisements slotted in or around children's programmes anything which might 'result in harm to them physically, mentally or morally, or which could take advantage of their natural credulity or sense of loyalty'. Such ads should not encourage a child, for example, to speak to strangers or go into a strange place to collect coupons; open fires shown must always have a fireguard, if a child is present in the scene; bottles of medicine may not be shown on a bedside table within reach of a small child.

The IBA's Code for Medical Advertising limits what may go into ads to simple palliatives for simple ailments for which self-treatment is safe. Any claims have to be of a restrained nature.

Making a commercial

Making a commercial may take anything from hours to weeks and cost anything from £1,500 to £100,000 (for a series). Scenes are frequently filmed over and over again – until the director is satisfied. Ron Fouracre, one of Britain's leading commercial directors, once shot a TV ad for a new animal magazine and reached 'take' 87 before he was satisfied – largely because a cat would not do what was wanted. Although the commercial only had to last 15 seconds, his crew used 1,200 metres of film at a cost of £450 for the stock and £500 for the processing.

One commercial for Nimble bread took a week to shoot in the mountains of Wales: the reason – the hot air balloon kept being taken in the wrong direction by eddies of wind. For that commercial, two cameras mounted in helicopters and a third in a Land Rover were used. The entire crew on location totalled 30 people including the actress 'star' whose contract required that she should not become airborne! So the owner of the hot air balloon was dressed in a woman's wig and white dress, matching the actress's colouring, and the camera took long-shots while 'she' was in the air. Close-ups of the real actress were taken in a specially-constructed replica of the gondola of the balloon, erected on a platform just above ground level.

All completed advertisements are viewed by the Advertising Control department of the IBA, and by the specialist staff of the programme companies. This is to make sure that the films are as the scripts indicated they would be, and that nothing has gone wrong in relation to the rules.

Then finally, the commercials are transmitted and the viewers see them for the first time.

Although there are over 20,000 new advertisements each year, due to ITV's strict advertising control policy only a handful of complaints are received.

Actual 'on air' costs depend, usually, on the size of the audience and time of day at which the ad is screened, although thousands of ads – public service films on health, safety and welfare put out by the Government – are screened free.

A shopkeeper who only wants to reach his local customers in Aberdeen or the Channel Islands needs only spend a few pounds. For the big national advertiser, however, who wants to be seen on every television set in the United Kingdom, advertising time can cost as much as £10,000 for 30 seconds.

Seen in perspective, these figures appear entirely acceptable to the advertiser. A single night-time broadcast of a network advertisement usually reaches 8 million homes and, at £1 for every 728 homes, the advertiser is able to attract attention in every seven or so homes for just one penny!

Chapter 7
The box in the corner

We see television as television because of a simple human weakness – our eyes are incapable of registering a tiny pin-point of light which is hurtling all the time back and forth across the screen. Instead of seeing it as a single moving spot, we see it as a series of thin, closely-spaced lines. We are not conscious of these lines, sitting a metre or so away from the TV set, nor of the fact that 25 separate pictures are being built up every second, each slightly different from the last.

This is because of another physiological mechanism known as the 'persistence of vision': it is the ability of the eye to retain, for a tiny fraction of a second, an impression of the shape, colour and brightness of an image after light from the image has ceased to be received. This 'decay time' of the eye is about 80 thousandths of a second.

Providing the pictures on the screen are built up faster than the decay time of the eye, the brain is spoofed into believing that it is seeing one, continuously-moving picture. The fast build-up occurs inside the major component of the TV set – the cathode-ray tube.

Inside your set

There are nine stages of 'blocks' to a modern 625-line colour TV set and more than 500 components altogether. In order of action, as the signal comes in, they are:

The tuner. Connected to the aerial, it permits signals on any channel to be selected, amplified, changed in frequency and then fed to

The vision and sound amplifier. This component strips the picture signal from the electro-magnetic carrier waves on which it has travelled from the transmitter. The accompanying sound signal is also amplified, rectified and passed to the loudspeaker of the set via a *sound output stage.* The 'clean' vision signal then moves on to

The video stage. Here the wanted signal – by now closely resembling the signal put out by the camera in the studio – is again amplified. Any colour information is de-coded and combined with the brightness information to produce three colour signals corresponding to the red, green and blue components of the original scene. The combined signals are then fed to

The picture tube. The tube is like a giant torch with a screen on which hundreds of thousands of tiny specks of phosphor have been neatly deposited; some red, some green, some blue. Variations in the incoming electrical signal are made to activate the phosphor in a pattern of brightness matching that in the original scene by

The scanning generators, otherwise known as 'time-bases'. These supply current to the coils which deflect the scanning beam back and forth across the phosphor deposits inside the tube. They are synchronised with those in the camera in the studio so that the pattern of light and shade on the TV set at home corresponds to that of the scene which the camera is looking at. The 'sync pulses' which do this job are separated from the rest of the incoming vision signal by

The synchronising separators, which, together with the *power supply unit*, make up the final blocks of the set.

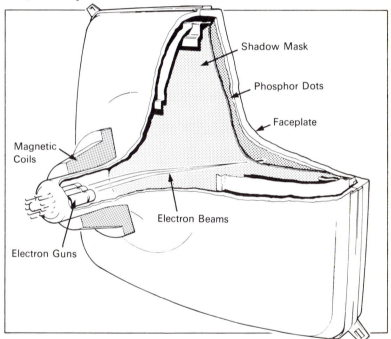

Colour TV receiver tube

Of all the components, it is the picture tube which is the most interesting (and expensive). The latest models measure up to 66 centimetres across the diagonal of the screen. Special quality glass is needed for the tube. It operates as a vacuum flask. Sucking the air out of it before sealing it imposes a force of several tonnes on the glass. The faceplate has to be completely free from blemishes and distortion and must not discolour under bombardment from behind by the electrons. Finally, the glass must be capable of withstanding scores of thousands of volts without electrical breakdown.

Inside the neck of the tube are three electron guns which 'shoot' streams of high-velocity electrons at the phosphor dots and make them glow. The beams are deflected from side to side and up and down by magnetic coils which encircle the neck of the tube at its forward end.

Behind the screen – two centimetres away from it – lies a metal plate punched with nearly half a million tiny holes. This is called the 'shadow mask'. It has the function of directing the streams of electrons precisely onto their targets.

Fashioning the shadow mask calls for precision engineering of the highest calibre. Holes vary in size down to 10 millionths of a millimetre and are tapered: they have to be positioned with an accuracy of less than a few thousandths of a millimetre across the whole of the mask.

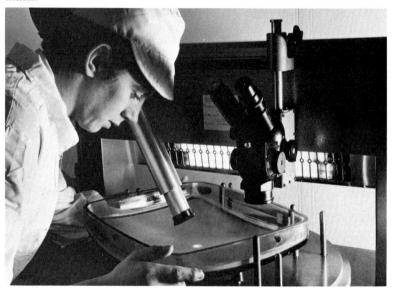

Checking the phosphor dots on a TV picture tube

The process used by Mullard Ltd – the largest manufacturer of shadow mask tubes in Britain – combines mechanical etching with photography. First, a sheet of mild steel is prepared as the basic material for the mask. It has to be scrupulously clean and coated with a substance which becomes hard when exposed to ultra-violet light.

Next, photographic negatives are prepared, each marked with 440,000 precisely-positioned spots. The negatives are clamped to either side of the steel sheet: one has slightly larger spots than the other but the two sheets are positioned exactly opposite each other, spots of one dead over the line of spots of the other. The whole array is then bathed in ultra-violet light before being developed in a photographic tank.

Where the spots were, the coating on the steel is dissolved. In all unspotted areas, the coating remains. So each side is marked with 440,000 little shallow pits, although the pits on one side are slightly larger in diameter than the pits on the other. These give the markings for the 'drilling' of the holes, which have to taper – hence the different sizes of the spots on the two sides of the plate.

The actual 'drilling' is done by multiple jets of ferric chloride solution. Both the strength of the chemical and the time taken over etching are meticulously controlled. The workers wear nylon overalls and caps and work in air-filtered 'clean rooms' because one speck of dust could ruin a mask by creating a mis-shapen hole.

The finished mask is inspected both electronically and visually. A photo-cell is used to check the size of the holes and the evenness of their distribution, for not only are they the guides through which the three electron guns will be firing their particles but they become the stencil, or 'master pattern', for depositing the phosphor particles on the screen.

The phosphor is generally deposited in the form of triangular groups of dots – one red, one green, one blue – each triangle being positioned in line with a hole in the shadow mask. Each dot is less than a tenth of a millimetre in diameter and must not overlap its neighbours. The groups are known as 'triads'.

When the tube is put together, screen, mask and the three electron guns are all lined up so that the angle of each beam of electrons is exactly right to carry it through the hole and land precisely on a phosphor dot of the right colour on the far side! Actually it tends to pass through about three holes simultaneously but it all happens 25 times a second.

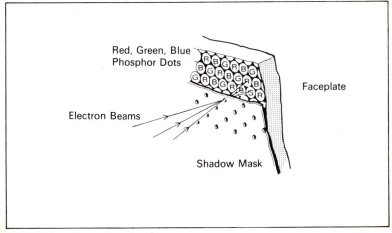

How a colour picture is produced

A TV picture in full colour is, of course, made up by mixing the three primary colours – red, green and blue – in different proportions. The 'mix' of actual colours is obtained by switching one or other, or two guns, off at a time. The coded instructions for this mix are contained in the signal leaving the studio and have to be unscrambled in the set at home. The appropriate electron guns have then to be switched on or off, literally at lightning speed.

There is one other aspect of the picture display which must be mentioned – 'saturation'. Saturation refers to the *intensity* of each colour and the degree of saturation in the PAL colour system (invented in Germany but adopted by Britain) depends on the amount of white light which is mixed with the colour.

The degree of pallor in a colour picture is adjusted on many British TV sets simply by turning one knob. But obtaining the correct adjustment of the three electron guns (to produce the right 'mix' of primary and secondary colours) is a much more skilled procedure and usually calls for an expert.

Correcting picture faults

When a TV set is sold or hired out, all the components should be working perfectly. But after some time, some parts – such as the automatic frequency control – may 'wander' a little due to ageing. If this happens, it may be necessary to adjust some of the external controls such as the 'vertical hold' or 'horizontal hold' to compensate.

You know that the 'vertical hold' knob needs adjusting if the complete picture starts moving up, as if it were turning on a drum: that is called 'picture slippage'. You know that the 'horizontal hold' needs adjusting if the picture is badly distorted and appears to be slipping sideways, or if parts appear to have been torn away.

By placing a mirror on a chair in front of the screen it is possible to observe the effect of making adjustments to the back of the set: but, a word of warning, turn the knob only fractionally, in one direction at a time. If possible, mark the starting point with a pencilled line so that you know how far you have turned. If the picture slippage does not correct itself, return to the starting point and try turning the knob slowly in the other direction. But keep pausing to check the effect.

Handling parts actually *inside* the set could be dangerous for an amateur and a qualified technician should always be called in. There are dangerously high voltages and certain types of radiation to contend with and, although these are limited by a British Standard, the safety margins may be less than satisfactory if the set is old.

Strict standards are laid down governing electric, magnetic and X-radiation levels. British Standard 415 covers not only radiations from scanning generators, video amplifiers and oscillators but also lays down limits for other safety aspects, notably the electric potential of exposed metal parts and temperature levels inside the set. Exhaustive tests are made by the manufacturers to forestall temperature rises because, if these do occur, they can cause the tuning to 'drift', the picture to shrink or alter shape, or the contrast to change.

It takes, on average, three hours to assemble a 625-line colour TV set. In 1975, they were being sold at the rate of 210,000 a month and the price of a 66-centimetre set was £260.

Thanks largely to the various rental systems, sales of television sets have mushroomed phenomenally during the last two decades. In 1950 there were no more than 5,000,000 sets in the whole world. Today there are nearly 300,000,000.

Mullard TV picture tubes

Chapter 8
The ubiquitous eye

The morning of 12 August 1960 dawned bright and clear at Cape
Canaveral, Florida. As night clouds scurried away, so searchlights
dimmed and the warm morning sun became the sole illuminator of a
tall, slender rocket, standing free of its gantry, half-way down the
Cape's line of firing pads.

'T minus One – on internal power.'

The metallic Tannoys echoed eerily from a line of poles stretching a
thousand metres from the pad to a mound on which 60 people were
huddled, binoculars at the ready, fingers fidgeting with cameras.

'T minus 15 seconds and counting.'

A hundred pairs of underground eyes flicked across figures and
scenes showing on monitor screens in a blockhouse barely a stone's
throw from the rocket. Another space 'first' was imminent.

'Ten, nine, eight, seven, six, five, four, three, two, one, ignition – lift-
off! We have lift-off.'

Telstar – still in working order

A fat tongue of flame and steam belched from the tail of the rocket as it hovered for agonising seconds above the concrete pad before rising evenly into the sky. Folded into its nose, with even greater fastidiousness than a parachute, were several tons of aluminised rubber – a giant balloon which engineers hoped to inflate as soon as the rocket reached space; a balloon with the appropriate code-name of ECHO.

A little later that day, ECHO became the world's first communications satellite – a 30 metre wide mirror, reflecting messages and crude pictures, beamed from one point on Earth to another. It was only an experiment. But it was followed, less than two years later, by a satellite specially designed to relay telephony and TV – Telstar.

Telstar is still in space and still in working order, although nobody uses it any more because technology has advanced to the point where its simple circuitry has become obsolescent – for colour transmissions something more elaborate is needed. But its impact on the Western world at the time was little short of sensational. A pop tune was even written about it.

Today, hardly a day goes by without some part of the nation's TV arriving via outer space. A chain of giant Intelsat satellites – each taller than a double-decker bus – relays not only pictures across the Atlantic but pictures from the Middle and Far East also: beautiful, clear pictures of a quality almost as good as when they impacted on the lens of some camera in a distant corner of the world.

The most widely-viewed television programme of all time was one which *originated* in outer space – man's first walk on the Moon. When Neil Armstrong and 'Buzz' Aldrin stepped out on 21 July 1969, their curious bunny-hopping walk was seen by an estimated 723 million people in 47 countries – and then seen by millions more through the medium of film or video-tape recordings passed on the next day.

Satellites played a vital part on coverage of that mission.

A satellite is basically an extension of the Post Office Tower – a relay station in the sky. Nothing stands in the path of the signal beamed up to it and nothing blocks the signal going down providing the ground stations are within line-of-sight of it and not over the curve of its horizon. To enable signals to reach stations which *are* over the horizon a chain of satellites is used, each relaying the signal on to the other. By positioning the satellites carefully, 36,000 kilometres up over the Equator, it is possible to match their travelling speed exactly to the spin of the Earth so that they appear always to 'hover' over the same point.

The satellite, of course, must take its operating power from the Sun. It collects solar energy with large panels of solar cells, linked to banks of storage batteries. Even so, very little of this power is available to the microwave transmitter inside the satellite and so the signal which arrives back on Earth is very weak – ·000000000000001 of a watt per square metre of ground. For this reason – especially since background noise is all the time trying to overpower the signal – it is necessary to have an Earth-station aerial nearly 30 metres in diameter. Britain's are located at Goonhilly Downs in Cornwall.

Satellites make available literally thousands of communications channels at a time and are in use, for the majority of the time, for telephony and telex rather than for TV: for this reason 'air time' through a satellite has to be booked and is expensive. To take in a report 'live' from its correspondent in Washington, during *News at Ten*, ITN may have to pay as much as £1150 for 10 minutes; collecting filmed despatches from the Middle East during the last Arab-Israeli conflict – relayed via a satellite positioned over the Equator – cost £1000 a minute.

Nevertheless the fact that satellites permit important events to be seen by a large audience *on the same day as they occur* has meant a lot to the TV news business and both the BBC and ITV spend heavily on satellite transmissions.

Taking in TV pictures from abroad via satellite is not a simple procedure. Different countries operate on different 'line' standards and have a different number of pictures per second to their transmissions. The US, Canada and Japan, for example, have 30 pictures per second, each picture being made up of 525 lines; Britain and Germany have 25 pictures per second, each of 625 lines. When pictures are exchanged between nations, therefore, they have to be converted to match the standards used by the viewing nation.

Until recently, this was done by positioning a TV camera in front of a cathode ray tube showing the incoming picture, but such 'optical' conversion resulted in considerable loss of picture quality. Now it is done electronically. The incoming signal is 'written' into electrical circuits which store the signal for a fraction of a second before re-assembling it at the correct speed and with the same number of lines as is required.

To convert incoming TV pictures to the British 625-line standard, engineers of the IBA have invented a machine called DICE (Digital Intercontinental Conversion Equipment). DICE converts information about the picture into digital form – it treats every line of picture as if it had 256 levels of brightness and then assigns a number to each level using a computer-type binary code. The waveform is then sampled 13 million times a second. So the US 525-line pictures, for instance, becomes a stream of figures to the machine – $525 \times 256 \times 13$ million $\times 30$ little pieces of coded information which have to be 'spread' across the 625-line British screen. Furthermore, the completed pictures have to be reproduced, without jerky movement, and at a slightly slower speed than the original camera worked at – only 25 pictures a second for Britain, compared with the original 30 a second in the USA. The processing takes place at tremendous speed: whereas a ray of light takes only one-seventh of a second to travel round the world, DICE has to perform each calculation in the time it takes light to travel 48 centimetres! Although the equipment is smaller than a wardrobe, it contains electronic components which do equivalent work to 16 million transistors.

Satellite systems provide for the simultaneous sound signal in addition to the vision signal. Sound circuits are also available in submarine cables. If the sound is transmitted separately via submarine cable it arrives early and has to be delayed by about one-quarter of a second to restore the correct time relationship between the two signals.

Cable transmission
Satellites, of course, are only one way of sending pictures over long distances. Cables are another.

There are two types of cable transmission system for sending vision signals. For short distances of up to about 18 kilometres the signals can be sent directly over a 'coaxial' or a 'balanced-pair' cable. A coaxial cable consists of a single conductor surrounded by a coaxial outer conducting sheath; a balanced-pair cable, as the name implies, is a pair of insulated wires enclosed in an outer screening sheath. For distances in excess of 18 kilometres only coaxial cables are suitable.

Much of the detail in a television picture is severely reduced when the signal is transmitted over a cable. This is due to various cable losses which increase with frequency and with the length of the cable.

Microwave relay
Over longer distances, microwave relay systems are used. These operate in the Super High Frequency range of the radio spectrum and are

Typical microwave link

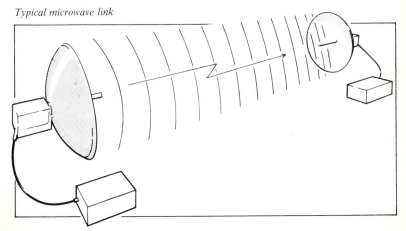

124 Television: Behind the screen

like fine, pencil beams of radio waves which travel like light. Transmitting and receiving aerials have to be in line-of-sight of each other and even when the 'dish' or 'horn' aerials are mounted on towers, the maximum distance that can be reliably covered in one hop is about 70 kilometres. For longer journeys, repeater stations have to be used.

Outside broadcasts

Both cables and microwave links are used for most outside broadcasts, within Britain and from overseas. Outside Broadcast units are completely self-contained. At the centre of the unit is a special van known as 'the scanner'.

The scanner is mobile technical centre and producer's control room, all in one. Pictures from all the outside broadcast cameras come into it and the producer/director assembles them into a programme which he despatches to Master Control back at the company's base. Sometimes more than one scanner is used.

One of the first all-colour, custom-built outside broadcast scanners went into action with Yorkshire Television in 1968. Measuring 10 metres long, 4 metres high and 2·75 metres wide, it weighed 13 tonnes and had three separate areas embracing the four major functions of a permanent TV studio – production control, sound control, vision control and a technical engineering section. It was fully transistorised and carried with it four cameras, each weighing 80 kilos, together with 24 microphone channels – it even had its own miniature automatic telephone exchange.

Commenting 'live' during Outside Broadcasts is usually a mixture of spontaneity and careful preparation. Commentators covering race meetings spend hours memorising cards showing the numbers of cars and the faces and names of drivers, or the colours worn by jockeys at the racetrack. The commentary has to be spoken into a 'lip mike' at just the right level, with just the right amount of enthusiasm and with no apparent pauses. There must be no 'fluffs', either about events, rules or people – literally millions of critical pairs of eyes and ears are liable to notice the error.

Outside broadcasts reach screens all over Britain via a network of cable and microwave links. And it is a similar but even more extensive network which brings Britain the bulk of her TV from abroad – via Eurovision.

Eurovision

The headquarters of the European Broadcasting Union, which is responsible for Eurovision, is located in Geneva. But its technical nerve centre is located in a series of attics above the Palais de Justice in Brussels – one of the tallest buildings in Europe. While lawyers and policemen bustle about in the great hall below, half a dozen engineers

The daily Eurovision news exchange – Margaret Hayes of ITN makes an offer

sit in the attics, observing banks of monitors illuminated with the call-signs of Europe's TV stations – 27 of them in 22 countries all belonging to the European Broadcasting Union (EBU). On to the monitors, at fixed times of the day, come the pictures of that day's happenings in Europe – perhaps an explosion in Belfast, a bank robbery in Paris, demonstrations in Lisbon, arrests in Spain, a Prime Minister receiving the Freedom of the City of London, the launch of a new space station by Russia, a football match in Munich.

The men are bi-lingual – they switch as easily from French to English as they flick programme material between countries. The material comes in from an aerial on top of the Palais, is switched, and goes out the same way. The network extends to every European country except Iceland (it has to fly its programmes in by air because it is too remote to pick them up direct) and takes in Tunisia, Morocco and Algeria. It also connects with Intervision – its counterpart in Eastern Europe – and with the Soviet Union.

Besides having a building with a dome rising 120 metres into the air, Brussels is ideally situated as the technical centre of European television. With a special aerial and slight modification to his set, the ordinary Brussels viewer can have a choice of eleven TV channels from five different countries!

Inasmuch as languages permit, many small countries rely on fellow members of the EBU for a high proportion of their entertainment material as well as for foreign news. This is usually because their budgets do not allow much original production.

Most of the programmes exchanged on Eurovision relate to sport. In 1970, for example, 518 of the 645 programmes exchanged were of a sporting nature and 90 per cent of all material was either sport or news. For the big international occasions, the European Broadcasting Union sends its own producers to the scene, making sure that the event is 'shot' or edited in a way suitable to its viewers. The EBU then bills its members according to the 'Rossi Scale' – a sliding scale of charges, invented by a Swiss banker named Rossi, based on the number of TV sets per country (the smaller nations pay less than larger ones but the quality of the service remains the same). It also arranges bookings of satellite air time and bills those wishing to receive the satellite material using the same scale.

The daily exchange of news items actually begins with a 'sound only' hook-up at 10.45 am of all stations. The technical centre in Brussels links a news editor at each participating station with the EBU co-ordinator in Geneva. A typical discussion may begin with a 'Good morning, *bonjour tout le monde*' followed by a list of any satellite bookings. Then the discussion is handed over to be chaired by one of the news editors, each country taking it in turn to be host for a fortnight. The chairman asks each country in turn what news film or video-tape recordings it expects to offer that day. Germany, for example, may reply that she has film of a new police radar device for checking the speed of cars; Italy may have film of the Pope inspecting his Vatican guard; ITV in Britain may offer coverage of a Press conference on the Loch Ness monster while the BBC may put forward highlights of a European Cup quarter-final soccer match. News agencies such as UPITN, Visnews or CBS may also contribute and, at the end, the co-ordinator works out a story list which is then sent by telex to each member country with a request to indicate by 1345 hours which items it wishes to receive.

As the day proceeds there are, inevitably, changes in the list: news is not always foreseeable and, also, not all the planned films or recordings materialise. The list usually alters slightly before the first exchange is made at 5pm. A second exchange occurs at 7pm for 'late arrivals' or for material transmitted by satellite from America.

Most of the material originates in the West. The amount of material actually used by any one country depends to a large degree, on how many foreign-based camera teams it maintains: in one typical year, Yugoslavia (which keeps no cameramen outside its boundaries) took 2,810 foreign items from the Eurovision network while Germany (which despatches camera teams all over the world) took only 528.

Sending crews abroad

The despatch of a camera crew to another part of the world is by no means a simple procedure and can be costly. The camera and lighting equipment are heavy and may run up a bill for hundreds of pounds of excess baggage charges on airlines, in addition to the fares of the crew. There are also Customs formalities to be gone through before film can be returned for developing. But there are few people working in television who do not look forward to foreign assignments and the creation of the EBU with its daily 'hook-ups', has made a big difference to the spirit of co-operation which is encountered by TV teams going abroad from Britain. As a rule, local personnel are exceptionally helpful to visitors and a high degree of camaraderie exists.

Having been both a newspaperman and a television journalist, I can testify to the fact that it is much easier to work abroad on TV assignments than on newspaper stories. The power of the TV 'eye' is ubiquitous.

Not all foreign assignments go smoothly, of course. Thames Television – whose reporting teams and camera crews travel more than a million kilometres a year – once had some valuable equipment stolen in South America, together with most of John Edwards' clothes. And most TV reporters have ended up, at some time in their careers, in one foreign city with their personal baggage or equipment mis-directed to another.

Sometimes – either to save money or because of a shortage of staff – TV companies hire the services of a local camera crew and merely send a 'front' man abroad. This can pose problems, especially in remote parts of the world where there is little television and the local 'stringers' may do other work besides operating a camera or sound recorder. The 'front' man is entirely at the mercy of the professionalism of the local crew.

The actual size of a TV team operating abroad depends on three things – the mission, the number of people available and any union agreements. Alan Whicker for his *Whicker's World* operates with a crew of between six and eight, including director and production assistant.

ITN crews rarely number more than three – reporter, cameraman and sound recordist – with a lighting technician added if the filming has to be done indoors. In such conditions, the reporter takes over the role of director and becomes responsible for the entire production (including, if he is wise, helping to hump the crew's heavy equipment).

An outstanding example of teamwork while filming abroad occurred on 20 July 1974. Michael Nicholson, Ray Moloney and Christopher Wain were in position in Cyprus, covering the mounting friction between the Greek and Turkish communities for ITN, along with two cameramen John Collins and Alan Downes, and two sound recordists, Bob Hammond and Tony Piddington.

Early on the morning of the 20th, a telephone rang in the Ledra Palace hotel in Nicosia. Peter Lynch, an ITN 'stringer', was on the line from Tel Aviv, passing on a tip from Peter Snow in London to the effect that Turkish regular troops were about to invade the island. The message indicated that the landing would be 'at Salamis Bay in the north'.

Michael Nicholson roused the others but it suddenly became obvious that the message had become garbled: Salamis Bay was in the south-east of Cyprus, not the north.

It was decided that Ray Moloney should go south, Michael Nicholson north and that Christopher Wain should sit tight in Nicosia. Despite the fact that it was 2am, Nicholson and Moloney managed to hire cars.

About twelve kilometres along the road from Nicosia towards Kyrenia, Nicholson's car broke down. Despite tinkering, it would not re-start and he, Alan Downes and Bob Hammond had no alternative but to unload their equipment and start walking back to Nicosia.

After some five kilometres of trudging, a BBC camera crew passed them, heading north, followed a few minutes later by another. Ribald greetings were exchanged as the BBC cars sped past, in the opposite direction. The ITN men's spirits were low. Suddenly, as they neared a village at about 4am, Nicholson heard the rumble of heavy aircraft engines.

On location – a Southern TV camera crew in Aden

They looked up to see Turkish paratroopers by the score dropping from the sky. Far from missing the action, they were in at the start of it.

It was 4am. The problem then became how to get the film back to Britain. 'We tried commandeering a Morris Minor,' explains Nicholson, 'but it belonged to a nurse. Then we saw a brand-new Volkswagen. That belonged to a lawyer. "Excuse us," we said, "but can we borrow your car to get some film to London? We're from British television." To our amazement he said "BBC or ITV?" "ITV," we replied. "Oh, that's all right," he said, "I used to work in London and I always watched *News at Ten*. Hop in."'

They set off in the VW, the owner at the wheel. But Turkish troops had set up road blocks. An officer told them to drive towards a camp and wait there. However, as the car entered a village, the three ITN men jumped out and ran down an alley to freedom.

Mortar bombs and shells began to drop around them as they tacked themselves on to a line of troops moving towards Nicosia. Eventually in another village, they found a restaurant owned by a Cypriot whose son managed a Wimpy bar in Neasden and they hid in the restaurant's ovens until the sounds of battle died away.

It was then about 1pm. They were only fractionally nearer getting their film to London but, to their amazement, the village where they were hiding suddenly became the second dropping zone for the Turkish airborne forces. Dozens of large helicopters, bristling with troops and guns, began landing 200 to 300 metres away.

Out came the camera again and some spectacular film was taken – 'a film director couldn't have positioned us better,' Nicholson said later. But heavy shelling started and once again the precious film became pinned down.

'Eventually,' recalls Nicholson, 'we got fed up and decided to run for it, dropping flat each time we heard a shell fired. You could hear them coming.'

Spaced about 10 metres apart, the three ITN men eventually reached Nicosia, walking openly down the middle of the road to the Ledra Palace hotel where some 200 other journalists had been confined since the invasion started. The next task was to record commentaries and type 'dope sheets', listing the sequences filmed and the footage of film used, to guide staff back in London. This was done in the hotel's cellars (upstairs, three United Nations soldiers had been killed).

It was decided that Chris Wain should make a run for it, using a borrowed car, and try to reach the British base at Akrotiri. Alan Downes and Tony Piddington volunteered to syphon petrol out of cars outside the hotel and they took the largest of the hotel's flags, draped it over the escape vehicle and cut holes as viewing ports.

Wain, Piddington and John Collins sped away waving white pillow cases, the precious film stashed away in another pillow case on the back seat.

Boldness is sometimes an ally and in the confusion of the invasion it paid off. Road block after road block waved them through, convinced that they must have permission – as they claimed – from 'higher up'. They had a further stroke of good luck when they reached Akrotiri to find an RAF VC-10 with its engines already running, about to take off for Brize Norton in Oxfordshire. The pilot agreed to take the pillow case.

A message was then telephoned to another ITN man in Cyprus, Alex Valentine, who was in direct contact with London from the Cypriot town of Episkopi. By the time the VC-10 reached Brize Norton, a chartered helicopter was standing by with one of the news editors, Mark Andrews, aboard – ready to rush the film to London – and two special editing teams had been assembled to prepare the film for that night's *News at Ten* bulletin. Being the first (and highly dramatic) film of the invasion, it had a major international impact and was sent – via Eurovision – all over the world.

There is one small footnote to this story of collaboration: as Andrews grabbed the pillowcase of film, a Customs officer at Brize Norton moved in. 'Is this import freight or passenger baggage?' he queried. 'Neither,' said the pilot, 'it's SHOP.'

'It's actually film from Cyprus for *News at Ten*,' added Andrews hastily, 'and we're in a desperate hurry.'

The Customs officer waved him on his way. Afterwards, he turned to the RAF pilot and asked, 'As a matter of interest, what's SHOP?'

'Ah,' said the pilot, 'it's a new piece of television jargon. It stands for Safe Hands of Pilot.'

Chapter 9

The future

So, what of the future?

In television, nothing stands still – least of all the technology – and some exciting developments are now taking place which promise to bring notable improvements and conveniences for the viewer in future.

For instance, 'The Box' itself is changing. It is becoming slimmer, easier to control, more versatile. Gadgets are being developed to make it do other things than provide entertainment. Eventually, it may occupy an entirely different place in the room.

The camera is changing – becoming smaller, more robust, lighter in weight, requiring less power, able virtually to see in the dark.

Production is changing. More and more subject matter is being put directly onto television, as opposed to film, and recorded, as opposed to being transmitted 'live'.

Transmission is changing. Instead of the signals being sent about the network in analogue form (in other words, in measurable waves) they may soon be travelling (along with telephone traffic, telex and computer data) as digits. Little high-speed pulses, crammed together in a kind of numerical code, which can be repeated along the link as often as necessary to bring the signals back up to strength and remove virtually all distortion.

The thinking behind television is changing too. The technical facilities to provide a fourth channel already exist and it may not be long before viewers are enjoying the benefits of one. It may also be possible, one day, to have programmes on demand – either down a cable from a central pool, using a coin-in-the-slot technique, or through lending libraries of video-discs or tapes.

The question is not so much 'What is coming?' but 'When?'

Imagine yourself in a comfortable centrally-heated living-room, dressed (for ultra-comfort) in a kimono, relaxing with a drink in your hand. Hooked onto the arm of your chair is a small box, about the size of a paperback novel, with buttons and knobs on it: it is the TV set controller. You need not rise from your chair to change the programme and, if you wish to know the time, the half-time football scores, the latest news headlines, or the weather forecast, you simply push a button or two on the hand controller. The information appears on the screen within seconds.

All that is already possible.

Now imagine yourself in the same room, in the same kimono, with the same drink. This time, the whole family has assembled to watch a re-run of *Upstairs, Downstairs* or of *The Forsyte Saga*. Instead of the usual quibbling and quarrelling over the positioning of the set – 'Harry can't see' – 'Now Jill can't' – the family is relaxed. *Everyone* can see because the screen is 125 centimetres wide and has come down from the ceiling.

That, too, could be with us soon. One day it may be possible to hang the TV set on the wall, or carry it outside and view it in brilliant sunshine.

Now imagine yourself as a TV cameraman, working the touchline of the Cup Final. Slung from your neck you have a small satchel; in your hand a camera no bigger than a power-drill. Twilight comes – but no matter: the floodlights are quite sufficient for your camera, which automatically adjusts to the lowering light level, giving clear, bright pictures to the viewer.

Such a portable, lightweight TV camera is but a year or two away and may well revolutionise outside broadcasts.

Our glimpse into the future shifts to the office. It is 6pm and the husband knows he is going to be late home. He rings his wife. No reply. He takes the telephone in his left hand, presses a button and dials a code. In a second, his phone is connected to the TV set at home. He dials out a message which begins to print out across the screen in the living room at home: SORRY DARLING BUSINESS CONFERENCE MEANS CANNOT BE HOME TILL TEN. He puts the phone down.

A few minutes later, his wife returns home. She reads the message and takes out a stack of plastic discs, each about the size of an EP, from a cabinet. She slips them into a playback machine and switches on the TV set. Within seconds she is watching (for the twenty-second time) her favourite movie, *Butch Cassidy and the Sundance Kid*.

A variety of inventions and discoveries have made all these hypothetical situations possible. How quickly they are introduced into real life depends, to a large extent, on economic factors and on a number of decisions which will have to be taken by those who control our broadcasting – in other words, by Government and Parliament.

Should there be more TV and, if so, how much more? Should it be in the form of a fourth channel? How should it be paid for? Should it be broadcast in the way that it is today, by regional transmitters whose signals can be picked up by individual aerials, or should it come into the home – along with several other forms of communication – down a cable? Or should *both* systems co-exist? Should programmes be available on demand, like the 'speaking clock' TIM, by dialling a number? Or should they be recorded onto tapes and discs and either sold or hired out from libraries?

Not wishing to sound like a one-man Annan Committee, I shall confine myself to *technical* considerations.

TV, until now, has been primarily an entertainment medium. Two-thirds of the material transmitted consists of sport, films, music, plays, serials, comedies and entertaining children's programmes: only one-third is classed as 'serious' and barely a tenth is news. But the TV set can now be used for other things – for the playback, as often as wanted, of any kind of recorded programme and for the display of printed information.

The question has to be asked, however, 'Who should control such things?' and which of the rival systems should be made available to the public?

Video cassette recorders

It is now possible to attach to the TV set a machine resembling a large stereo record-player which will both record a TV programme 'off air' on to a cassette and replay it – or any similar cassette of video-recording – at any time of the day or night.

Three such 'video cassette recorders' were available in Britain in 1976. Two of them are really miniature versions of the larger video tape recording machines used at TV studios. They have helical scanning heads and record onto either half-inch or three-quarter inch tape. They give up to 60 minutes of recording time on a single cassette, although the cassette has to be turned over after 30 minutes so that both 'tracks' can be used. Tapes can be erased and used again – up to 300 times.

When J. Stewart-Clark, then Managing Director of Philips Electrical Ltd, launched the first of the two systems in London on 18 August 1971, he began his speech by saying 'Welcome to the biggest event in television since television!' He went on to forecast that, by 1980, something like 2 and a half million homes in Britain would have video-recorders by 1980 and that their price would be 'less than the price of today's 66-centimetre colour television'.

It could still happen. But by 1976 fewer than 15,000 had been sold and the price of his Philips machine – the latest is known as the VCR N 1501 – was still £550 (compared with £350 for a 1972 66-centimetre colour TV set). Slow buying may be blamed on the country's general economic recession, but – as with Baird's first TV sets – public interest proved difficult to arouse.

The second video cassette recording machine – the Sony U-matic VO 1810 – was even more expensive (although far more sophisticated). Instead of coming down from its 1975 price of £765, it actually went *up*. Even the third – National Panasonic's video cartridge recorder – was costing £595 as this book went to press. Furthermore, the blank cassettes or cartridges for these machines cost anything from £14 to over £20 for an hour's recording.

As a result, the use of video recorders, up till now, has been

confined largely to educational, industrial and commercial organisations who may wish to make training tapes or test advertisements or
monitor TV programmes 'off air'. Nevertheless, there is little doubt
that, ultimately, a very large number of homes will have them.

Some people in the television production industry cannot wait for
this to happen: they believe that the effort put into the making of
many programmes deserves a second – or even unlimited – showing.
Others are not so sure. They point out that, if the cream of TV can be
skimmed off and kept in store at home, the viewer is likely to become
far more discriminating about what he or she wishes to see 'live' on
the screen. This could have an effect on audience figures and, thus, on
the level of advertising. Furthermore, the question of artists' 'repeat'
fees becomes crucial (at present, many performers collect at least a
percentage of their original fee if a programme is repeated). It may be
that the various unions concerned will seek a higher initial fee – to
cover the *possibility* that the viewer may replay the programme at
home.

Negotiations have already started over performing rights for other
forms of TV recording. For, once the equipment – and it does not have
to be a *recorder* but may be a simple playback machine – has been
installed in the home, other possibilities arise.

Thousands of movies, drama series, comedy shows, documentaries,
sports lessons – even degree courses – are now being lined up for re-
recording so that they may go on sale, be rented out or placed in TV
'libraries' and then played back through the home TV player. Nobody
has really taken the plunge yet and produced large stocks because it is
uncertain which system will have the most popular appeal. For, in
addition to video-cassette and video-cartridge, there are also video-
disc and video-film machines.

Video-discs

Ironically, it was John Logie Baird who, in 1927, invented the video-
disc. One of his originals – resembling a large, metal gramophone
record – is permanently on view to the public at the IBA's Television
Gallery in Brompton Road, London. But Baird was unable to get
enough signal information into the grooves of his disc to produce
anything better than a crude picture on his screen.

Today's video-discs produce clear pictures, but at a price.

There are at least six different systems under development, but only
one so far on the market – and that one, called 'TeD', only in
Germany. TeD looks very much like a record player except that the
records (video-discs) are made of flimsy pvc and are slotted into the
front of the machine still in their wrappers – special cardboard
envelopes. The whole machine is attached to the home TV set by a
special adaptor. The discs themselves measure 20 centimetres across

Video disc – the TeD disc gives 20 minutes of recorded TV

and are etched with microscopically-fine grooves – about 30 grooves to the width of a human hair, laid down in a spiral. The grooves, which are really V-shaped troughs, carry the picture and sound signals up their sides in the form of undulations. The whole disc revolves at a speed of 1500 revolutions a minute, riding on a cushion of air. Across the grooves, riding gently over the undulations like a motor boat, travels a diamond stylus on a lightweight pick-up arm which is driven slowly across the record by a thin wire belt. In other words, instead of the stylus riding *in* the grooves, as with a musical LP, it is driven *across* them – picking up the signal information on the way. This is known as 'pressure scanning'.

A disc may be played at least 1000 times before any deterioration of the TV picture occurs. Colour is good and the TV set needs little adjustment – far less than with a cassette system. But in Germany, where TeD playback machines were first marketed in March 1975, the asking price was 1498 Deutschmarks (about £280) and each 20-minute disc cost between £2 and £5. In other words, were a full-length Hollywood movie to become available, the necessary stack of discs might cost the home viewer as much as £50.

Obviously, costs will tumble once mass-production begins. But who is to say what should be mass-produced? A rival organisation, MCA, an off-shoot of Universal Studios in Hollywood, is currently trying to arrange for 11,000 old movies to be put onto video-disc. But whatever is offered will have to be something which convinces the viewer that it is worth paying extra for subject matter which he cannot get on his screen in the normal way. The first 180 video-discs marketed in Germany offered German-language programmes on hobbies, sport, physical fitness training, plus cartoons and children's programmes – hardly riveting stuff and certainly not the kind of material which would make *me* invest £300 or so in the equipment. Furthermore, there are artists' performing rights to be considered before realistic price lists can be issued; and there is the possibility of rival systems, working on different principles, coming onto the market.

TeD is the product of a group which includes the British firm of Decca and its main rival in Britain, when marketing finally goes ahead here, is likely to be Philips, who have a video-disc system under development called VLP – Very Long Playing. Their disc resembles a music LP except that the television is recorded onto it in the form of tiny, oblong pits, which are pressed into the plastic surface. The variation in length of the pits and their spacing gives the information

Video disc – the Philips VLP

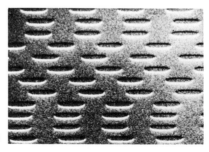

*Close-ups of the pits in which
TV signals have been recorded*

needed for playback and scanning is done, not by the stylus, but by a moving spot of light (provided by a laser). Up to 45 minutes of playing time is possible.

The system (and American systems like it) is so different from the TeD principle that the two types of disc will never be interchangeable. Should both be marketed?

Telecine player

And should rivalry be allowed to develop between video-cassettes, discs, cartridges and yet another system – 'Super 8' film?

The 'Super 8' film player – a miniature telecine machine which can be attached to any 625-line TV set – permits colour or black-and-white film to be played back directly onto the screen or recorded onto video-tape for playing later (in its latter role, it can transfer the filmed image onto magnetic tape through any kind of video-tape recorder in existence today, including all of the home video recorders). The first one marketed for general use was introduced in 1975 by the German firm, Normende.

Normende's telecine player takes standard 'Super 8' film on conventional open reels which are loaded into a cassette. The film is automatically fed into the player and, after a maximum playing time of 30 minutes, is automatically rewound. The cine film is converted to a TV image by a flying spot scanner.

This play-back technique has several advantages over conventional projectors. Film runs continuously through the telecine, instead of jerkily as in a projector, giving better sound quality. The telecine has no sprockets to engage the perforations in the film, thus reducing wear. Normende claims up to 2,000 plays without damage to the film.

Once again, the drawback is price – £950, in the case of the Normende machine.

Should all these systems be allowed to compete, in the way that disc, cassette and cartridge have in the music industry? Or will the rivalry have the effect of making the public hold back, thereby keeping prices high? We can only wait and see.

Laser beams and glass fibres

But there is an alternative. New technology is opening up the possibility of carrying as many as 2,000,000 vision channels directly into the home. The secret is to use glass fibres and to put the picture information onto the backs of laser beams, then shine the beams down the fibres and de-code them in the home. If so many channels can be offered, then it might be possible to assign several thousand of them to 'stored' TV programmes, held centrally in a video-library, and give the viewer access to them via some kind of dialling device in his living room. He may pay for what he wants with a coin in a slot, or possibly by subscription, but a catalogue of what is available, plus a price list, would allow him to make a selection at any time of the day or night.

The question then arises: 'Who should operate such a service?' Local authorities? The BBC and/or ITV companies? Private groups of commercial firms? As one American observer put it 'The broadcaster's nest has not been deeded to him in perpetuity. The pressures for change within the next decade could force the established broadcasting company to reform its ideas about programme delivery, or find itself playing to a diminishing audience. The broadcaster's role as a programme packager could turn out to be far more important than his control of a communication channel. New technologies could turn his world around.'

Perhaps the last word on this subject, for the moment, should come from Admiral Lord Mountbatten. When, as Chairman of the National Electronics Council, he opened the IBA's Television Gallery on 25 September 1968 he said: 'The few television channels compare unfavourably with the number of Press outlets. I think we need more varied and free-speaking television sources, particularly on the educational side. Among the entertainment channels, I would like to see "Pay Television" – this is a way of paying for television which makes a lot of sense to me. But this is not to denigrate the achievements of both the BBC and ITV: one cannot travel round the world without realising that British television is head and shoulders above any other country's television service.'

Digital signalling

Widening the choice of TV programmes for the viewer may well depend on a number of developments now being assessed by the British Post Office. By introducing new techniques for transmitting signals about the country – both nationally and locally – Post Office engineers hope, eventually, to give millions of people access not only to more entertainment sources but to a range of information services such as have only been dreamed of, until now, by science-fiction writers: computers for supplying knowledge; automatic letter-writers for delivering mail into the home overnight; document transmitters and photo-copiers; telephone directories, train timetables, hotel reservations, tips for self-diagnosis of simple medical ailments, tax return guides, home courses for students, message services – all via the TV screen, or by some other visual display unit located in the home.

The key to many of these things is the perfection of 'digital signalling'. Digital signalling means converting the information to be transmitted – whether it be speech (as in a telephone conversation), pictures (as in photographs or TV), or typed characters – into a kind of pulsed code which can be sent at high speed and interpreted automatically at the other end.

Up till recently, most forms of communication have involved using 'analogue waveforms'. Sounds or pictures leave the originating source as waves – waveforms which have an infinite number of shapes and amplitudes or, in other words, an infinite number of variables in them. Signals corresponding to these waveforms are known as 'analogue signals' and they take a lot of sorting out.

At present, the electrical signals sent out by a TV transmitter are directly related to three things – the brightness of each part of the picture, the degree of saturation of the colour and the loudness of the sound. The signals are *analogous* to the originals – in other words, they exactly correspond to the original values. Their amplitude fluctuates continuously, of course, and measurements of the fluctuations are made continuously. They emerge as a series of peaks and troughs, like waves in the sea, and the sizes of these peaks and troughs are transmitted as a series of numbers, which are then converted back into waveforms in the TV set at the receiving end.

But engineers have come to realise that they do not need all this continuous information in order to get a clear result at the other end – that it is possible to summarise it and so reduce the number of signals which have to be sent out. It is a little like the children's drawing game where by joining up numbered dots a picture can be built up. In the case of the TV picture-of-the-future, the brightness, colour intensity and sound levels will be assigned individual values according to a binary code: as the picture is scanned, so a kind of numerical precis will be made of it and the information turned into a sequence of digits. Each picture will become a stream of numbers, which will leave the transmitter at the rate of 120 million digits a second, like high-speed Morse.

Equipment at the other end will follow the numbers and turn them back into colour TV pictures.

The same 'digital' technique can be used to summarise speech on the telephone, or to condense the information in a photograph, drawing or typewritten document so that these, too, can be transmitted over distances. Once the information is in digital form – in numerical code – it can be manipulated in some interesting ways.

It can be re-generated, for a start as often as necessary. Repeater stations can be positioned at intervals so that, whenever the signal is growing weak, a fresh set of digits can be generated (matching the original) at full strength. Distortion should then become a thing of the past.

Secondly, the information can be compressed. Different types of transmission can be switched in together – telephony with TV, fac-simile with telex, telex with TV and so on – to make maximum use of the 'air time': after all, it is only sequences of pulses which are being handled, like with like.

The Post Office sees all this mixed information zipping about Britain via new forms of communications links – invisible beams, hollow tubes and glass fibres.

The invisible beams will be microwaves of even higher frequency than those in use today. The hollow tubes, called waveguides, will be laid in trenches beside roads and across fields. The glass fibres will be bundled together and pulled along existing telephone cable ducts. Down these various channels – each having advantages and disadvantages over the copper wires and radio beams in use today – will go not only telephone and TV signals but computer 'talk', facsimile information and electronic message-writing.

The screen at home, in the view of the Post Office, will become not only a source of entertainment but a fact box and message pad also.

Oracle and Ceefax

In a sense, it has already become a fact box, although comparatively few people are yet able to use it as such. The facts are made available through a new system for displaying information on the TV screen called 'Teletext'. There are two forms of 'Teletext', one invented by engineers of the IBA, the other by engineers of the BBC. Since both are similar in principle, and have since been made totally compatible, I shall confine myself to explaining the IBA version, with which I came into contact at a very early stage.

CEEFAX – putting information in

ORACLE – how the information looks to the viewer

The IBA system is called ORACLE. The word ORACLE is an acronym for Optional Reception of Announcements by Coded Line Electronics. At present it gives the viewer an option of receiving up to 800 'pages' of information – written facts about TV programmes, the weather, news, sports results, market prices and so forth – any of which he can bring onto his TV screen at the touch of a few buttons.

All that is needed to give the viewer this optional extra is a small array of electronic components called a 'de-coder', which is fitted inside the TV set, and a hand-controller. The hand-controller is a small box, about the size of a one pound box of chocolates, with 14 buttons on its face, each bearing a number from 0 to 9 or a title such as 'hold' or 'text'. The viewer keeps it by his chair.

He also has a directory listing all the services available through Oracle – and the relevant 'page' numbers.

Page 200, for example, contains the latest news from ITN. To get it – or rather, a written summary of it – the viewer simply pushes the buttons marked 'TV and Text', or the one marked simply 'Text' on his hand controller, followed by those numbered 2, 0 and 0. Within seconds, a summary of the news appears on the screen. It appears either over the existing picture (if the 'TV and Text' button has been pressed) or over a blank screen (if the 'Text' alone button was used).

The words appear as lines of white (or coloured, if preferred) characters with a maximum of 150 characters to a 'page' – equivalent to about 10 centimetres of a standard column of newspaper print or a 45-second radio bulletin. A typical ITN news summary may occupy several 'pages' and the viewer simply pushes buttons to make 201, 202 and so on, until he has read through as much of the news as he wants.

The first advertiser to use Oracle for a quick cry for help was the Surrey and Hampshire Canal Society whose members during the summer of 1975 urgently wanted volunteers to help unclog a canal. They got a few and, afterwards, one of the Society's officials commented, 'It will certainly be a great day when anybody starting out on a canal holiday can dial up the appropriate page of Oracle and get up-to-the-minute information regarding lock closures on any part of the canal system, or can dial another page to check on times and heights of high water around the coast.'

The first experimental transmission of Oracle information began from the IBA in April 1973. Public transmissions began two years later. All news was fed in by a special ITN unit operating from the eighth floor of the ITN building in Wells Street and all other information was handled by a team of four full-time staff and three part-timers at London Weekend Television's studios on the South Bank. These two units serve the whole ITV network. By January 1976, 500 of the possible 800 pages had been filled and were being regularly up-dated. The information is now being fed continuously into a computer which generates the necessary TV signals over the network.

The way Oracle works is by using four of the topmost 18 lines on the TV screen to receive the information and then 'rolling' this information down across the screen so that the viewer can see it.

Normally, on a properly adjusted set, the top 18 of the 625 lines which make up the picture are either blacked out or masked and the eye ignores them. But engineers have always used these lines (known in the trade as 'field blanking lines') to pass technical information around the network – signals indicating such things as the technical quality of the circuits or which studio originated the programme. What Oracle does is to fill four of these lines with coded signals which tell the cathode ray tubes in the sets of those who have 'de-coders' how to behave.

The electron guns inside the tubes are told when to activate certain combinations of phosphor dots behind the screen so that characters flash up instead of the original background of the picture. It looks like 'overprinting'. In fact, it is cancelling out – or rather, replacing – tiny cut-outs of colour with white, or one colour with another (if vividly-coloured display of the text is preferred to the basic white lettering).

The printed text appears as lines of white or coloured characters which quickly ripple across the screen and then 'freeze' until either another page is selected or the viewer reverts to the ordinary TV picture.

For the purposes of the display, the 'de-coder' (mounted inside the set by a qualified mechanic) instructs the electron guns inside the cathode ray tube to consider the screen as being composed of 960 tiny rectangles – 24 rows of 40. Groups of phosphor dots inside these rectangles can be activated, with tiny margins of space around them, when the necessary instructions (in the form of coded signals) arrive from the nearest ITV transmitter.

The de-coder contains three or four large scale integrated circuits which store the incoming signals for a while and then use them to generate characters across the screen in response to a 'command' from the hand-controller.

Up to 24 lines (containing a total of 150 characters) make up an Oracle 'page'. The top line always displays the word 'ORACLE', gives the subject matter and number of the page, and shows the exact time.

And the price of Oracle? At the time of writing, only 50 or so units were in existence and the price of a de-coder was being set around £230, plus a further £20 for the hand-controller. But by 1978, the price is expected to drop to £100, plus £15 for the hand-controller – bringing Oracle within the reach (especially if rented) of hundreds of thousands.

Viewdata

Oracle and Ceefax, revolutionary though they are, may not be the ultimate in information systems as far as television is concerned. For, once Post Office engineers have developed their new communications links, they plan to link the TV set to the telephone.

By the 21st century it may not only be possible to 'dial a programme' and summon written information onto the screen at will, but also to use the TV set as part of a home computer terminal – and as a message pad also. It may be possible to use it to 'shop around' shops.

On 25 September 1975, at an international computer engineers' conference at Heathrow Airport, Sir William Ryland, Chairman of the Post Office at the time, announced: 'The day when people at home or work can call up information they need over the public telephone network and have it presented to them quickly and cheaply on a television screen is not so far distant.' He then unveiled an information system developed by Post Office research engineers called VIEW-DATA.

Viewdata has many similarities to Oracle and Ceefax in that information can be summoned onto the TV screen using a hand-controller with buttons, but a device called a 'modem', containing logic circuits and electrical components, links it to the telephone and allows pulses sent over the telephone lines to deliver the information to the screen.

The Post Office intends to supply the information from a network of computers – some national, some regional, some local – and make the user pay for it on his telephone bill. For this reason, it is likely to be considerably more expensive to use than Oracle and Ceefax, which are broadcasting all the time free. On the other hand, Viewdata has a capacity for an almost limitless amount of information.

Typical applications envisaged for Viewdata include:

Information Services
Telephone directories, yellow pages, transport timetables, what's on at local entertainment centre, weather.

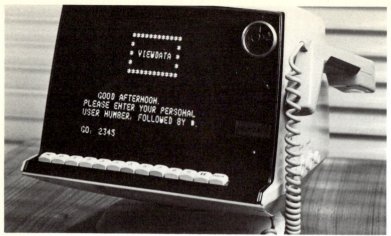

Proposed VIEWDATA home terminal

Hotel and Travel Reservations
Business Applications
Payroll, accounting, secretarial services, tax return preparation.
Education
Home courses for school-age children, specialised training courses for adults, link with 'University of the Air'.
Medical
Self diagnosis, local doctor/hospital medical services.
Professional Information and Services
Literature retrieval, technical information, report preparation and editing.
Shopping Aids
Shopping and mail-order services, market prices at local stores and supermarkets.
Message Communications
Link with Telex service, messages for absent customers.
Computing Services
Electronic 'slide rule', transfer of data and programmes between computers.

Because it can be made to respond to *any* telephone dial, no matter how far away, Viewdata will enable a person *outside* the home to generate a message across the screen *inside* the home simply by dialling the appropriate digits to make the words appear.

Thus the 'Sorry Darling I shall be late' warning on the TV screen from a husband at the office becomes practicable.

The first limited trial of Viewdata was due to start in 1976. The Post Office gave the description of how it would work:

'To get Viewdata information, users would first switch on the TV set and then call up the service over the phone by pressing a button on the control unit. They would not even have to lift the telephone receiver. Then, at another touch of the button, the Viewdata opening display – an index listing the subjects on which information is available – would appear on the TV screen. Following simple instructions displayed on the screen, users would select the information they wanted by pressing further buttons. The display would be cut off, and the call ended, also at the touch of a button. As an alternative to the telephone link to a domestic television, business users could have a purpose-made Viewdata terminal, with built-in controls and telephone.'

It is the Post Office's intention that outside organisations will provide the data for Viewdata's network of computers – public utilities, local newspapers, commercial firms and so forth. Because the system is likely to carry a great deal of classified advertising, a number of local newspaper groups have expressed considerable interest in the project – and they may well handle the ads on behalf of the Post Office.

In addition to small ads, the Post Office envisages Viewdata handling 'details of all the film shows, theatrical productions, concerts and ballet performances, recitals, ice spectaculars, wrestling and boxing matches and other entertainment and sporting events currently available throughout the UK just under one heading "Going out".

'Simple sketches, diagrams and maps could also be displayed on Viewdata, while colour gave added impact to both words and drawings. Up to seven colours could be used.

'It is also possible for users to send simple messages to each other over Viewdata,' the Post Office adds. 'Once the message is sent, it can be stored in the system until the person it is intended for is available.'

Eventually, the 'message pad' potential of Viewdata could have a major effect on telegram, telex or even postal services for it may be faster and more efficient to send text via the TV screen.

The objects of the 1976 trial are said to be 'to determine the range of information to be provided, establish charges for the service, and assess the likely demand. This would be followed by a full market trial towards the end of 1977 and a full public service could start in 1978–79.' But will the public be willing to pay for it?

The Post Office remains cautious on the subject of charges. But, in a leading article written in October 1975 after the first public demonstration of Viewdata, the journal *New Scientist* stated, 'The cost of Viewdata is likely to be high. The customer will probably have to pay a "surcharge" for a licence for a teletext TV, an installation fee for connection of the set to the telephone network, and rent of the equipment and his or her code number that gives access to Viewdata. Then he or she would be charged for each call (as for an ordinary telephone call) as well as a fee for the information viewed (except that provided as a public service by local or national government).'

The article went on, 'The Post Office would probably be responsible for billing, since to let the information providers know who had looked at their information would be an intrusion of the customers' privacy. It seems likely that Viewdata will be very slow to get off the ground.'

As I said earlier, two key factors in the spreading and cheapening of information services of this type are the perfection of 'digital signalling' and the development of new communications links.

'Digital signalling' calls for the use of integrated circuits for processing the signals and a whole range of new electronic components containing these microscopically-small circuits is beginning to appear. Known as 'processors' and 'micro-processors', they contain no moving parts and should therefore be more reliable and also cheaper to mass-produce. Automatic test equipment can be installed to monitor their behaviour. New types of exchange and switching centres become feasible and it should be possible, in many places, to use the same transmission equipment for generating TV, telephony *and* data – thus enabling equipment to be built in larger quantities and, again, at lower cost.

In television, digital signalling can be introduced at several points down the chain from studio camera to home receiver. Already, line-standards converters (like ITN's DICE machine for converting American TV pictures to British standards) use digital techniques. The next stop may be to have digital TV tape machines – giving almost perfect reproduction – followed (in the 1980s and 1990s) by the whole of TV production and transmission 'going digital'.

The result should be a considerable improvement in the quality of the picture on the screen, an opportunity for the viewer to have stereo or even quadraphonic sound, and access in the home to extra programme material or information channels.

But Howard Steele, the IBA's Director of Engineering, pointed out at an international meeting of communications engineers in 1974 that, since digital equipment might cost up to 25 per cent more than the analogue equipment in the early stages, the change-over to digital transmission would probably have to wait until the analogue equipment (in which about £500 millions has been invested in Europe) had reached the end of its natural life. The switch might take 15 years.

Once again, technology seems to have outstripped the economy.

Some of the new communications links to which I referred earlier may be delayed for the same reason. Although more and more people want access to more and more TV and information services, the problem is how to provide them economically.

Microwave links

The Post Office is hoping to introduce improved equipment for relaying television about the country on the backs of microwave beams. TV is not the Post Office's sole concern of course (radio, telephony, telex, facsimile transmission and the routine exchange of computer data are equally in demand), and the key to carrying all this extra information about the place is to raise the frequency of the carrier wave.

Technically, this is not easy. Whereas TV is radiated directly from the transmitter mast to the home at frequencies of millions of cycles per second (MegaHertz) microwave relay links (used for linking the whole country onto the TV network) have to operate at frequencies of *thousands* of millions of cycles per second (GigaHertz).

At present, they operate at 6 GigaHertz. But if experiments now being carried out at the Post Office Research Centre at Martlesham in Suffolk are successful, new equipment will be installed (much of it small, simple horns or 'dishes' on the tops of poles) which will operate at frequencies of 18–19 GigaHertz. Given approval to invest in the 'pole-top' microwave links, the Post Office should be able to offer far greater carrying capacity than is possible today – perhaps up to three TV programmes per microwave link, or 20,000 two-way telephone conversations – and distortions should be eliminated by using 'digital signalling'.

Microwave waveguide

Even more ambitious carrier systems are under development.

One of the problems with microwave links is accurate alignment of the transmitters and receivers – not only do both have to be in line-of-sight of each other but they have to be angled very carefully so that the radio beam carrying the TV signal lands fair and square in the aerial cup. Vibration and swaying of the mast may cause distortion, as may bad weather. One solution is to send the beams down a tube or 'waveguide' – rather than through the air – and this is what Post Office engineers are now trying to do.

Microwave waveguide looks like a straight copper tube, five centimetres in diameter and very shiny inside. In fact, the interior of the tube is wound with a spiral of fine copper wire, the windings being laid with extreme precision. Air is sucked out, after sections of the tube have been joined together, so that a vacuum is created inside. Signals are beamed through the vacuum.

A single five centimetre tube, it is estimated, should be able to carry 200 TV circuits simultaneously, or 300,000 telephone calls. More elaborate systems may be able to carry up to 1,000 TV circuits. It will also be possible to use the same frequency in different waveguides – easing the crowding of the frequency spectrum and eliminating co-channel interference.

An experimental microwave waveguide, 14 kilometres in length, is now in operation between the Post Office Research Centre at Martlesham and the nearby town of Wickham Market. Television test pictures, beamed in at one end, show virtually no loss of quality at the other, despite the fact that the tube has carried the beam around several corners and bends. The tubes are laid in trenches beside roads and across fields and the idea is, eventually to build a whole network of them linking the main centres of Britain.

Once waveguide transmission has been perfected and the tubes installed on a massive scale, it may be possible to dispense with most of the masts and towers at present used for broadcasting TV and use those instead.

Fibre optics

Another alternative would be to use light as the carrier for the signal, instead of radio waves. Or the two may be used in conjunction with each other.

Light beams are already being tested in the laboratory. Post Office engineers are trying to develop a system for distributing signals locally, using as few amplifiers and booster stations as possible. And if they succeed, literally thousands, or even millions of TV, telephony, telex and facsimile channels will become possible into the home.

The idea is to use lasers to generate the light beams, modulate them with TV picture and sound information, and then send the treated beams down thin strands of glass, which will conduct them wherever needed. 'Piped' TV and telephone calls would be the result, the 'pipes' being strands of glass no thicker than a human hair.

The new technique is 'fibre optics'. The glass fibres are totally reflective inside. None of the light beam or signal escapes out of the side and – because very pure glass is used as the core – there is very little weakening of the signal, even when it is conducted round bends.

The strands of glass have to be manufactured very carefully, each strand consisting of an inner core and an outer coating or 'sheath'. Glass of a different refractive index is used for the outer coating – in other words, the formulation of the glass which forms the sheath is such that light will not shine through it but will travel instead along the core of clear glass in the middle. Yet both core and sheath are fashioned in the same hot crucible and are pulled out as one fine strand, outer coating clinging to inner.

Television in the distant future, therefore, may well travel by a combination of routes. Some of it may still go through the air, radiated in the ordinary way: but most of it will probably go by tube – over long distances – and then by glass fibre into the home. And because the frequency bandwidth of laser light is so much greater than that of radio energy, something like 2,000,000 channels for TV become theoretically possible into the living room. There could be, in theory at least, an unlimited choice of programmes or recordings.

It was this prospect which led me, in 1969, to invite Tony Wedgwood Benn and two electronics engineers to a series of lunches in the Charing Cross Hotel in order to investigate the practicality of using the TV set as a voting device. Tony Benn had made a speech mentioning the idea of an 'electronic referendum' – a technical system by which the public could indicate its feelings on issues of the day at frequent intervals: in this way, he believed, a lot of individual frustration would be relieved and national tension lowered.

We devised several possible forms of referendum, ranging from questionnaires delivered through the mail (the cheapest way), to measuring surges of current at power stations resulting from lights being switched on ('yes') or off ('no') in response to voting invitations broadcast over the radio or TV. Finally we invented 'Friday Night is Voting Night' – an all-TV system in which the voter would watch television programmes outlining the issues of the week and then press the 'yes', 'no', or 'don't know' button on his set, while a studio 'audience meter' was indicating the nation's feelings.

Technically, it would be possible: whether any government would allow it is doubtful.

The future TV set

What other developments can we expect in 'The Box' itself? Well, the most immediate will be in the cathode-ray tube. Instead of perforating the 'shadow mask' with hundreds of thousands of *round* holes, most masks will soon be cut with slits instead of holes. The advantage of using slits is that it will make it easier to converge the three colour images – red, blue and green – exactly over each other on the screen. In the past, two separate sets of components, known as convergence coils, have been needed to overlay the colours precisely all the way across the screen. Furthermore, when the present set is moved about, there has been a tendency for the colours to drift apart and a technician then has to be called in to adjust a number of knobs inside the set. The slit shadow-mask tube uses fewer components and the colour – once converged at the factory – should not drift.

Another development, which came onto the market in 1975, is a 'freeze-frame' facility for 'The Box'. It allows the viewer to 'freeze' any TV picture for closer examination later – perhaps to discuss a point of football, or to take down an address.

At present, it takes the form of a special modification to the whole TV set, but later it may prove possible to offer it in the form of an attachment. The first of the modified sets was announced by Matsushita Electrical Industrial Co of Japan.

In addition to conventional circuitry, Matsushita's modified set contains a storage tube, which is switched on to extract a still from the screen and then switched again to display the still. The tube actually stores the waveform for a single frame of the TV picture. This can be read out on to the screen over and over again.

The 'frozen' frame is displayed as a rectangle in the corner of the screen while the rest of the screen shows the continuing programme. As a refinement, the viewer can zoom in and out of the still picture to make small writing, for example, more readily visible. The position of the still on the screen can also be controlled.

Another recent development is in the controls of the TV set. Quite apart from the hand-controller for Oracle and Ceefax, a number of firms are currently introducing control boxes which can be operated from the armchair. One of these works by activating a tuning fork – vibrations travelling from the fork through the air are picked up by a small receiver in the set and used to switch to another programme. Others have a more elaborate ultra-sonic transmitter inside.

Flat TV

Then there is the screen itself – scientists are trying to make it larger and flatter. At present, the size of screen is limited by the angle through which electron guns in the cathode-ray tube can 'spray' electrons from side to side as they activate the lines of phosphor dots which make up the picture. At present, the maximum angle is 110 degrees and the largest domestic screen is 66 centimetres across the diagonal. But research teams are working hard to develop much larger screens, using novel projection systems, and even a new kind of 'flat' TV set which may be thin enough and light enough to hang on the wall.

One way to make the picture larger is to project it onto a screen which is separate from the set. One such system, the Sony VPP 2000, has a 127-centimetre screen which can be positioned anywhere from three to 20 metres from the viewer and a box-shaped projector on castors. Announcing its development, Sony declared that it offered group viewing of TV 'at a substantially lower cost than with TV projection systems available to date'.

Even so, in 1976 it cost £1,495. A larger system, the Sony VPK 1200E, which projects through lenses onto a screen measuring three metres (across the diagonal), was priced at £15,000. Obviously it will be many years before projection systems of this type come within the means of the ordinary viewer, although they can be of considerable value to businesses, industrial firms or educational establishments.

An alternative approach is not to use a projector at all but to make the actual elements of the screen glow by running an electric current through them. In this way, it would be theoretically possible to have a screen of unlimited size.

Several companies are now working on 'mural TV' or 'flat TV', as it has come to be known. The TV receiver would be no thicker than a dinner plate.

In 1968, the Radio Corporation of America announced that it had taken a vital step in this direction. The key, it suggested, was the growing of 'liquid crystals' whose ability to reflect light could be readily changed by running an electric current through them, and it demonstrated several devices in which this happened, including an all-electronic clock with no moving parts and a thin box displaying a high resolution, still picture which looked like a TV test card.

'Liquid crystals' are hybrids which occur frequently in Nature. They are organic compounds with properties of ordinary liquids – they pour like water – and they have an ordered crystalline structure like quartz. They are transparent.

They are made up of millions of tiny, cigar-shaped molecules, lined up neatly like matches in a box. When current is introduced, the molecules are 'scrambled' and the transparent crystal becomes frosty, due to light scattering. When current is shut off, the crystal instantly becomes clear again.

The RCA team was able to produce 'liquid crystals' which remained stable and could be electronically controlled over a wide temperature range. Coupled with advanced electronic circuitry, crystals would operate at near room temperature in a TV set.

In the devices demonstrated, the letters, symbols and numbers remained stationary. Engineers explained that, to display motion, the crystals would have to be assembled into a very fine mosaic of some 330,000 elements, each of which would have to be 'scrambled' or 'unscrambled' 30 times (or, in the case of British TV, 25 times) a second.

The electronic circuits and tiny components needed to achieve this high-speed 'scrambling' are still the major obstacle to 'mural TV' and a practical system for the home still seems decades away.

By 1970, Sony researchers had reached the stage where they could demonstrate moving television pictures on a flat 'liquid crystal' screen measuring 10 by 14 centimetres and Hitachi scientists had a system working with a 12 by 18 centimetre screen. The first contained 560 elements in its mosaic, the latter 280. Small though these displays were, it would seem possible to enlarge them by slotting the whole display into a slide-projector and projecting onto a wall – although some loss of picture quality would be bound to occur.

A different approach is to use electro-luminescence – EL for short. Possibly the best known EL device is the compact night-light which plugs into a wall socket and glows a dim but reassuring green. Green is the colour usually associated with EL, but scientists have developed variations in the phosphors used in EL and can now produce other colours, including white.

In an EL television screen, the electro-luminescent phosphors are laid out in neat rows and sandwiched between strips of transparent electrodes. The strips criss-cross to form a matrix. The phosphor cells which run vertically are connected to strips in front of them, those running horizontally to strips behind. To get a particular cell to glow, a voltage is applied across two strips. It is rather like locating a street corner in New York on a map. 'Fifth Avenue and 42nd Street' means the intersection between the two streets: 'Vertical column electrode 73 and horizontal column electrode 231' means the phosphor deposit lying at the junction of those two strips and indicates where the voltage has to be applied to produce the luminous effect.

The first electro-luminescent 'mural TV' was demonstrated by National Panasonic in 1968. The screen was less than five centimetres thick but only measured 32 centimetres across the diagonal and the number of phosphor cells blinking on and off to form the picture – 52,900, laid out in 230 lines – was far too few for enjoyable viewing. Mitsubishi followed this with a slim-screen with an even smaller number of lines – a mere 80. Since then, EL television has remained locked in the research laboratory.

In April 1975, a British consultant in electro-optics, Martin Tobias, writing in the journal *New Scientist*, summed up the position like this:

'Five years ago it was popular to talk about the possibility of the flat-screen TV. Pundits reckoned it would be widespread by the mid-1970s. So, whatever happened to it? Well, to be frank, it has arrived . . . in several research laboratories around the globe. If one classifies video displays capable of displaying several lines of images or alpha-numeric characters as TV displays (even though they may not as yet possess the 625 by 640 point resolution of broadcast-TV images), then no fewer than eight different technologies have so far produced flat-panel TV displays – one, at least, in full colour.

'Why does anyone bother? The cathode-ray tube (CRT) is cheap, reliable, can outpace human vision, and paints pictures and alpha-numerics in glowing colour. Although TV sets are not yet truly pocket-size, many occupy little more volume than, say, a portable typewriter. And with an estimated world-wide total of more than 262 million TV screens, there is clearly enormous capital tied up both in the CRTs themselves and in their manufacture.

'It must be acknowledged that there is at least one "good" motive for development of a flat-panel replacement: a convention CRT display is tiring to watch because of flicker from the scanner. At least some of the flat-panel alternatives eliminate this. Other, more doubtful, benefits – such as a screen viewable simultaneously from both sides, or a display that could be inserted into a slide-projector for bright, wall-size pictures – may also result.'

But *when* is still anybody's guess.

Three-dimensional TV

So, if we are not likely to have 'flat' TV in the near future, may we have 3-D TV? Once again, the answer has to be 'Perhaps, *some* day ...'

In the 1960s, a former BBC engineer put forward an idea for 3-D television which would involve the viewer in the use of a pair of special spectacles, containing one red and one blue lens.

The idea, which was put forward by M. G. Maxwell, now working with Kriesler Australasia Proprietary Ltd, New South Wales, was to view the scene in the studio from two slightly different angles in the same way as it would be viewed by the two eyes of a human being in the studio. The scene, as viewed from each angle, would then be transmitted through separate channels to the viewer's home. There the two angled views would be displayed separately.

'Separate transmissions of the two scenes would be achieved by transmitting them alternately. The normal 50 frames a second would be transmitted, but 25 of them would be of the scene viewed from one angle and 25 of the scene viewed from the other. The left- and right-hand viewing lenses of the camera would be placed six centimetres apart to represent the normal spacing of human eyes. Both lenses would illuminate a single black-and-white colour television camera, but the signal from the left lens would then modulate what is normally the red carrier of the colour television signal transmitted from the station. The right-hand lens signal would modulate the blue carrier. In the viewer's home, the red signal would produce a red picture and the blue signal would produce a blue picture.'

The main drawback to Mr Maxwell's idea was that the viewer, wearing his spectacles, would only see the scene in black and white. More sophisticated systems, now at the research stage, may one day permit 3-D viewing without the use of spectacles – *and* in colour – but there are still enormous technical problems to be solved.

The basis of them is a technique known as holography.

'Holography' literally means 'the whole message'. It has been described as the visual equivalent to hi-fi stereo in music. In holography, light from a laser is split into two beams. One is pointed at the scene to be photographed or televised, the other (called the 'reference' beam) at a mirror. Light reflected from both beams is mixed to form a hologram – a jumble of so-called 'interference patterns' which looks blurred and meaningless to the naked eye until another laser is shone onto it from the back. Then, it suddenly springs to life and becomes a perfect 3-D reproduction of the original.

Holography, in the form of still pictures, is now in use commercially

– amongst other applications is one for establishing the exact time of death in murder cases. But its use in television is held up by the problems of converting the 'interference patterns' into TV signals and mounting – safely – a laser or lasers in the home receiver.

It may never happen – on aesthetic as well as technical grounds. For, as Dr Boris Townsend of the IBA's Engineering Division put it: '3-D television gives the viewer the impression of looking down a tube at some action going on at the far end. It makes figures on the screen seem unreal – almost like painted puppets. This doesn't seem to occur when looking in two dimensions.'

TV games

So, what other extras may be added to 'The Box' in future? One possibility is to play games on it.

In the July 1974 issue of *Practical Wireless*, full instructions were given for adapting the home TV set to play 'Teletennis' – a similar game to the one now widely installed in pubs and restaurants.

The game can be plugged into any 625-line television aerial socket (colour or black-and-white) and the court outline displayed on the screen. A 'ball' is served at the press of a button, and two 'bats' are operated by the players.

A more sophisticated game was described in the July 1974 issue of *Television*. 'Tennis', 'football' or 'golf' can be played with either colour or monochrome receivers. When the football game is connected to a colour television set it can display a green football pitch, touch-lines, goal posts, and red and blue players. The players can be moved anywhere on the screen and can 'kick' hard or gently and even give some 'flight' by swerving the ball.

Morris Colwell, editor of the magazines, calculated that the simplest of the games could be made at home for something like £30 – and still can.

The future of the camera

Apart from 'The Box' itself, in what other areas of television may one expect advances in the future? Well, undoubtedly, there are major developments ahead for the TV *camera*.

The TV camera-of-the-future, one can now say with confidence, will be no more bulky than today's 8mm home movie camera. It will require only a small satchel of ancillary equipment to operate out of doors, and it will be able to operate virtually in the dark.

The key to this development is a miniature electronic component called a Charged Couple Device (CCD) invented by two American scientists early in the 1970s. A CCD is basically a compact nest of electronic circuits and detectors built up on tiny 'chips' of silicon. It replaces today's bulky camera pick-up tube, with its electron gun and deflector coils, by a component no bigger than a matchbox. The image at which the camera is looking is allowed to fall directly onto the electronics which, in turn, can be 'interrogated' electrically, section by section, at fantastic speed. A CCD camera still needs a system of lenses (which make up most of its bulk) and electronic components to 'interrogate' the Charged Couple Device, but these can be much smaller and need a power supply of tens, rather than thousands, of volts.

The first CCD cameras are already in action in spy-in-the-sky satellites. Others are about to go into use in specialised industrial roles. It may be a decade or two before they begin to displace today's plumbicon or vidicon tubes in entertainment television (the TV networks have invested heavily in the conventional equipment and, in any case, today's cameras are quite good enough for studio purposes) but a change-over will surely come, especially in outside-broadcast cameras. The massive back-packs in use in 'roving eye' TV cameras today – such as those seen on the touchlines during sporting events – will become things of the past. Furthermore, because of the extreme sensitivity and efficiency of the CCD as a means of storing picture information, the camera will be able to operate almost in the dark: it will be possible to monitor what is happening during, say, the siege of a house in which terrorists have been cornered almost as easily at night, or in darkened conditions, as in daylight.

CCD cameras, which are extremely reliable, are already carrying out 24-hour surveillance from outer space. Others are being developed for monitoring battlefields – the device can be made to look at the enemy lines at regular intervals and notify an operator if anything has moved since the last look – and for steering shells. A CCD TV camera has been made small enough to fit into the nose of a shell so that the gunner can see, literally, where his shells are landing and alter the course of subsequent rounds if they are off target.

Other CCD cameras are being developed for bank and supermarket surveillance, for medical use and for checking markings on banknotes or pill-bottles. One interesting application is for juggernaut lorries. Where the driver previously had difficulty in gauging the distance between the back of his lorry and an object towards which he was reversing, he can now watch a monitor screen in the cab and see what is happening with the aid of a small CCD camera on the tailboard.

The first detectable result of this improvement in camera technology, as far as the home viewer is concerned, will probably be clearer TV pictures under bad lighting conditions – winter sporting events, dusk or night-time scenes in news bulletins and so forth. But the miniaturisation of the camera – and its new robustness – may lead to familiar objects being shown from unusual angles and to the camera probing the nooks and crannies of some we have never seen before.

The lightness and reliability of the CCD camera is likely also to accelerate the trend towards putting more and more material directly onto television, as opposed to film, and to lowering the lighting requirement at the production site, although, as I said earlier, the next decade may have come before this happens on any significant scale.

The future of satellites
What else?

Well, experiments have started in America using satellites to broadcast television directly into homes or communities on a wide scale. A number of communications satellites are due to be launched in 1976–77 for this purpose because, over a massive land-mass such as the USA, it is cheaper to relay it in this way than by using ground links.

A satellite has also been positioned over the Equator to relay educational TV to thousands of villages and schools in India. Mexico also intends to use satellite television for educational purposes. India has a population of nearly 500 million, mostly spread about in 550,000 small villages, and the idea is to position 3-metre diameter receiving 'dishes' in as many of these villages as possible so that inhabitants can be taught and informed via the medium of a few TV sets placed in the village hall or hut.

Engineers have estimated that a satellite-borne education system for the whole of India might cost £6,000,000 a year to maintain and operate over a 10 year period, and £2,000,000 a year in Mexico – only a fraction of the cost of installing cables or microwaves.

Whether such a system would ever be introduced in Britain is questionable. The idea was dismissed by the Government's Television Advisory Committee in 1973 on grounds of cost. The committee pointed out that if conventional receivers were used, the transmitting power of the satellites would have to be of the order of tens of kilowatts and 'this will not be feasible for a very long time indeed. Lower power could be used if modified receivers were employed but the modifications would cost about £80 a set. The cost over a 10-year-period would be of the order of £100 million for the broadcasting side alone. The bigger cost would be for modifications to home receivers: this would run to hundreds of millions of pounds.'

However, there are many attractions in switching to such a system. Ultimately, it will become possible to broadcast directly from satellites into individual TV and radio sets in homes and classrooms anywhere on Earth, without the need for intermediary ground stations.

The ultimate will be a master grid which can be linked to a system of computerised information storage, and by means of which every person on earth will have access, at any time, to any information he may require.

Through such a grid, a student in a small college could tap the resources of a great university overseas. A country doctor could get help from a distant laboratory or teaching hospital. A government official on one continent could draw on the accumulated experience and wisdom of older governments in another part of the world to assist in preparing modern legislation. A famous teacher could reach with ideas and inspirations into far off classrooms, so that no child need undergo the neglect of mediocrity.

These are some of the technological miracles of communications just ahead.

The pity is that, as Howard Steele put it in his Faraday Lecture, 'probably never before in the history of television has there been so much innovation and development in the pipeline – yet all of it, no doubt, will in due course be taken for granted.'

Acknowledgements

I should like to thank especially Janny Aird, Malcolm Beatson, Tom Hadley, Alan Hawkins, Norman Hooper, Mike Neusten, Howard Steele and Dr Boris Townsend for their considerable help with this book.

Peter Fairley

The publishers would like to thank the following for permission to reproduce the photographs in this book:

Associated Newspapers, page 66; *BBC Photograph Library*, pages 17, 22, 32, 54, 140; *EMI*, page 135; *Malcolm Goy*, pages 38, 39, 47, 50–1, 55, 61, 63, 86, 88, 135; *Susan Griggs*, page 125; *Independent Broadcasting Authority*, pages 100, insert 103, 106; *ITN*, pages 88, 125; *Mullard Ltd*, pages 116, 119; *Philips*, page 136; *Post Office*, page 144; *Press Association – Reuter*, page 120; *Roger Scruton*, page 71; *Southern Television*, page 128; *Thames Television*, pages 67, 69, 73, 77, 79, 141; *TVTimes*, pages 13, 15, 48, 81, 91; *Yorkshire Television*, page 103.

In addition we would like to thank *ITN*, *Thames Television* and *World of Sport* for their co-operation.

Cover photograph shows Thames Television studio, Teddington.

Further reading

Adventure in Vision. John Swift. John Lehmann Ltd. 1950.
Basic Television Part I. H. A. Cole. The Technical Press Ltd. 1967.
BBC Handbook. Published annually by British Broadcasting Corporation.
Beginner's Guide to Television. Gordon J. King. Hamlyn Publishing Group Ltd. for Newnes Books. 1958.
The Focal Encyclopaedia of Film and Television Techniques. Focal Press. 1969.
ITV – 1968 – 75. Independent Television Authority.
Broadcasting. Garry Lyle. B. T. Batsford Ltd. 1973.
The History of Broadcasting in the UK. Asa Briggs. Oxford University Press.
The Physics of Television. Donald G. Fink and David M. Lutyens. William Heinemann Ltd. 1961.
The Technique of Television Production. Gerald Millerson. Focal Press. 1961.
TV and Radio. Independent Broadcasting Authority. 1976.
The Universal Eye. Timothy Green. The Bodley Head.
Your Book of Television. Norman Wymer. Faber and Faber.

Index